A COMMON LAND,
A DIVERSE PEOPLE
Ethnic Identity on the Prairie Plains

Edited by
Harry F. Thompson
Arthur R. Huseboe
Sandra Olsen Looney

The Nordland Heritage Foundation
1987

Library of Congress Catalog Number 86-61609

ISBN 0-9615558-1-5 Softcover
ISBN 0-9615558-2-3 Hardcover

First Edition
First Printing

Cover: *Dakota Road* by Carl Grupp

The Nordland Heritage Foundation
Box 2172, Humanities Center
Augustana College
Sioux Falls, South Dakota 57197

Publication of this book was made possible in part by a grant from the South Dakota Committee on the Humanities, a state program of the National Endowment for the Humanities.

 **PINE HILL PRESS**
Freeman, S. Dak. 57029

CONTENTS

Ethnic Identity on the Prairie Plains

*HARRY F. THOMPSON, ARTHUR R. HUSEBOE, AND
SANDRA OLSEN LOONEY*

The nine essays that follow explore and celebrate a fundamental
irony of the Prairie Plains — and American — experience: a diverse
people in a common land. The essays were originally presented
as papers at the Berdahl-Rölvaag Lecture Series (Nordland Fest),
the Seminar for South Dakota Humanities Scholars, and the
Augustana Journalism Forum — all held at Augustana College
between 1984 and 1986. The Humanities Seminar was held in
conjunction with the observance of the 125th Anniversary of
Augustana College in 1985. Represented in the collection to varying degrees are the following ethnic groups: Norwegians, Germans, Germans from Russia, Frisians, Irish, and Sioux. The
first five essays consider the European immigrants; the last four
essays focus on the Sioux. The theme of ethnic diversity/identity
is explored not so much by any one essay as by the combination
of perspectives the collection as a whole provides.

The Prairie Plains region, or flat grasslands of the northern
interior (Smith 2), is multi-cultural. At least as early as
14,000 — some archaeologists say 38,000 — years ago, nomadic
hunters from northern Asia followed animal herds across the
Bering Strait into the Yukon Valley and down onto these grasslands
(Zimmerman 49-51). In the intervening centuries, many travelers —

1

primarily Asian and European – have crossed this land in search of food, safety, or the fulfillment of dreams. One of the earliest recorded appearances of Europeans on the Prairie Plains occurred in the 1730s, when the La Verendryes encountered the Mandans and Arikara along the Missouri River (Zimmerman 18). Although the Sioux are considered by many historians to have migrated west onto the Prairie Plains as late as the mid-eighteenth century (Schell 20), recent developments in ethnoastronomy, for example, seem to confirm traditional Sioux belief that they were performing religious ceremonies in the Black Hills involving the alignment of the sun and stars as early as 3000 years ago (Evans 7). In the last third of the nineteenth century, Europeans began to settle on the Prairie Plains, displacing many of the descendants of those prehistoric immigrants. Though once separated by centuries, oceans, and languages, these travelers from diverse lands have found a common home and heritage on the Prairie Plains. Yet their distinctive cultures remain intact and enrich the region.

Robert Bly's contribution to the examination of these cultures is a combination of reading and commentary that supplied creative variety to the 1985 Humanities Seminar at Augustana College. True to his craft – and to his eminence as a National Book Award winner – Bly declares war at the outset on sloppiness in language and then proceeds to illustrate his commitment to poetic precision with a series of readings from his own verse, from contemporary Scandinavian poets, and from rarely heard lyrics in Old Norse. As an aid to the listener (and reader) Bly offers short prose prefaces and afterwords that tell how he happened to write each poem and what each Scandinavian or Old Norse poem means. The eleven pieces by Bly and the nine old and new Scandinavian verses printed here form a miniature anthology that demonstrates the range of Bly's poetic interests. Although the themes of several poems relate to the topic of the 1985 seminar, most apropos is the short piece entitled "Moving Books to a New Study," for it leads Bly to deplore the cultural loss suffered by Norwegian-Americans when they exchanged their warm, spiritually enriching Norwegian culture for its American counterpart. Characterized as it is by isolation and loneliness, American culture does not do very well, says Bly, "in feeding the thirsty souls of old people—or young."

When Norwegian immigrants moved into the Sioux River valley in eastern South Dakota in the 1860s and 1870s, they clustered together in small settlements for companionship and mutual support in the struggle for survival in a harsh climate. While that pattern was the standard for pioneering groups of many nationalities in the northern prairie states, the Slip-Up Creek Settlement northeast of Sioux Falls takes on added interest because of its central role as the locale of *Giants in the Earth* and the other prairie novels of Ole Rölvaag. Historian Clarence Berdahl has a special interest, however, in the settlement beyond its value as a representative example of immigrant life on the Dakota frontier: his sister Jennie became the wife of Rölvaag in the Slip-Up Settlement on 9 July 1908, and little Clarence turned the ice cream freezer all that afternoon during their wedding reception. Moreover, Professor Berdahl's account of one family's migration from Norway in the mid-nineteenth century, with its attendant uncertainties and afflictions, is an outline of the experiences that many immigrant groups underwent, including the agony of separation, the hardships of the journey, the temporary settling in an established community, and the final journey into the unknown promise of Dakota Territory or elsewhere in the West.

Dr. Ruth Alexander treats three waves of South Dakota women writers from Territorial times to the present who give shape and form to the pioneer heroine. In fact and imagination, the pioneer heroine is a woman challenged by the wide expanse of prairie and sky, loving the freedom that the land and the pioneer community can give. The authors and their works—Borghild Dahl, in *Karen,* Mary Worth Breneman, in *The Land They Possessed,* Verna Moxley, in *Wind 'til Sundown,* and Marian Castle, in *Deborah*—picture strong heroines, worthy counterparts of the strong pioneer heroes. Both the pioneer hero and the pioneer heroine defined western settlement. Alexander states that women writers, frequently writing for young readers, drew upon a traditional theme in their depiction of the pioneer heroine—initiation into adulthood, coming of age. South Dakota women writers are "compelled to tell the story—a liberating story—of a young

3

woman's discovery of herself in the leveling atmosphere of a Dakota frontier setting." Alexander contrasts the more confined image of "true womanhood" of the nineteenth century with the liberating image of the pioneer heroines who were not bound by delineated spheres of activity. Alexander's "The Pioneer Heroine as Idea: South Dakota's Women Writers 1940-1970" introduces little-known writers and works important to bringing the image of the women on the prairie frontier into focus.

A counterpoint to Dr. Alexander's overview of strong heroines in prairie fiction is the masculine perspective provided by Frederick Manfred in "The Mystique of Siouxland," a transcription of his talk to the humanities scholars of South Dakota in 1985. In this reminiscence, Manfred recounts experiences from his Frisian upbringing in northwest Iowa and from his life on the Prairie Plains of Minnesota and South Dakota. For Manfred, home was magical. There he had heroes—his father, his uncles. There he learned to read tales of adventure—the Bible, *Giants in the Earth*. There he witnessed the Sioux caravans and unearthed an ancient Indian burial site. There he discovered a descendant of an aristocratic English family who had been banished to America under the dictates of primogeniture. Manfred named the Prairie Plains of his boyhood Siouxland, an area that provides the setting for his most famous novels—*The Golden Bowl, This is the Year, Lord Grizzly, Conquering Horse,* and *Green Earth.* In this talk, Manfred demonstrates that he is an enduring advocate of the land that has given him both physical and imaginative vitality.

The most authentic remnant of German culture on the Great Plains—the German language—is alive but not well, warns Dr. Paul Schach. True, some Mennonite and Calvinist communities in Kansas, Nebraska, and South Dakota continue to speak in their ancestral dialects. "Indeed, in one Sutton [Nebraska] Reformed Church," Schach writes, religious services are conducted exclusively in German even today." But such linguistic longevity is threatened by the forces of conformity. For example, Schach points out, the German spoken in the Hutterite *Bruderhofe,* preserved for decades by geographic isolation and ethnic homogeneity, is being eroded by public education and agricultural

4

manuals. Professor Schach's special concern, as expressed in this essay, is that the rich variety of ancestral German dialects be preserved for study by future scholars. Schach calls for the recording of "as much dialect material as possible as soon as possible, for this precious part of our ethnic heritage is rapidly disappearing."

The second half of the collection, which focuses on Native Americans, begins with Professor Ronald Robinson's consideration of white perceptions of American Indians, especially the spurious identity ascribed to them by the press. In "Idols of the Tribe, Idols of the Theater: Reporting on Native Americans," Robinson addresses the issue of journalism's acceptance and even advancement of Indian stereotypes. Employing Sir Francis Bacon's terminology for cultural preconceptions—idols of the tribe—and for professional preconceptions—idols of the theater—Robinson explores journalism's portrayal of *others*. For Robinson, idols of the tribe are the attitudes toward land, time, and giving. "The press . . . has not been able to cross the bridge between cultures, has not been able to transcend the idols of the tribe in order to establish the empathy required for effective communication," charges Robinson. Idols of the theater are attitudes about timeliness and prominence. As Robinson points out, journalism is reluctant to perceive Indian issues as new or of star quality. Robinson warns that "if the media sit waiting eagerly for some spokesman to arise, for something to happen that can get the message across in two minutes on the evening news . . . then there seems little hope for progress in the reporting of Indian affairs." The news media, asserts Robinson, are comfortable with the identity they have given to the Indian, and, like the society they represent, they fear the Indian when he is stripped of their cultural and professional preconceptions.

In "Women of the Circle," Virginia Driving Hawk Sneve addresses the difficulty of information-gathering about Dakota/Lakota women. She points to oral tradition and the winter count, transmitted by men and later recorded by men. The tribal experience recorded was mainly experiences affecting the male. Using these written records with their scant information to support her oral sources, Sneve interprets the experiences of the

5

women of the circle from prereservation times to World War II. The Dakota/Lakota women have had to adapt to painful adjustments in status. The role of the prereservation women was one of hard physical labor, yet status was accorded them. With the coming of the fur trade their status began to deteriorate. On one hand, the Indian woman was regarded as the Indian princess, but, more generally, she was considered a physical laborer, an economic commodity. In their own eyes, however, as Sneve tells from her oral sources, *women* and *motherhood* always remained synonymous terms. Sneve discusses white-Indian marriages, first among the fur traders, later among the ranchers and farmers who came to homestead. Such marriages produced further role and status changes for the Indian wife and her mixed-blood children. Sneve speaks of the shame that came as the women were traded for liquor to soldiers and passed among white military officers as spoils of victory. She tells of the women becoming the center of the circle defining Indian life as reservation settlement began, the isolation of the reservation allowing them to maintain traditional customs of homemaking and child-rearing. As Sneve joins oral history to documented records, the women of the circle walk with pain and fortitude the precarious path to the reservation.

In "Community and Tradition in Native American Society," Dr. Donna Hess defines values as "standards of desirability that people develop in relation to the experiences that they have in the world around them." For Native Americans, such as the Sioux, the community of experience determines the degree to which they hold to traditional Native American values. Four essential values of traditional Dakota life — bravery, fortitude, generosity, and wisdom — grew out of the community of experience of the Sioux. These values, however, were radically altered by the reservation system. The culturally homogeneous Indian community of prereservation times, the extended family, gave way to the heterogeneous community of missionaries, traders, soldiers, and government agents. The erosion of the traditional Sioux value system was exacerbated by federal boarding schools and federal relocation programs. The result has been the formation of a diverse set of values among the Sioux. Contemporary Native

Americans, whether they live in the rural, reservation world or the urban, non-reservation world, experience danger, uncertainty, and ambiguity. Yet, for Hess, the traditional values still are relevant in both environments.

In "The Pipe and Cross" Father Martin Brokenleg examines the results in modern Lakota society of the century-long interaction of two vastly different cultures and religious traditions. While Lakota religious life was essentially unified during the pre-contact days — centering as it did on the seven rites described by Black Elk and others — the beginning of reservation life on the northern Plains saw the gradual replacement by Christianity of that religious core. This substitute religion and the culture it carried with it continues to cause problems of adjustment today among the Lakota.

With the passage of the Native American Religious Freedom Act in 1978, however, there began the re-establishment of traditional religious practices among many Lakota Indians. Although Christianity had come to be woven into the lives of most of them, this new development has raised for the Lakota and indeed for all Native Americans new questions of religious values. Father Brokenleg identifies the four groups among the Lakota and the four practices that have arisen as responses:

1. those who want only traditional religion,
2. those who are exclusively Christian,
3. those who combine the two practices because "they see no difference," and
4. those who combine the two for the sake of unity.

As a result, a remarkable diversity of religious expression exists for the Lakota. Today our nation and the entire world, says Father Brokenleg, face "the same question of uniformity for the sake of peace, or diversity at the risk of war." The Lakota response provides us with the example of how one society has dealt with that challenge.

WORKS CITED

Evans, Gaynelle. "In the Alignment of the Sun and Stars, Scholars Read the History of the Sioux." *Chronicle of Higher Education.* 1 Oct. 1986: 7,9.

Smith, James Richard. *Geography of the Northern Plains.* National Council for Geographic Education Slide Presentations. Lincoln: Great Plains National Television Library, 1984.

Schell, Herbert S. *History of South Dakota.* Lincoln: U of Nebraska P, 1961.

Zimmerman, Larry J. *Peoples of Prehistoric South Dakota.* Lincoln and London: U of Nebraska P, 1985.

Norwegian Roots on an American Tree

ROBERT BLY

Robert Bly, of Norwegian-American descent, lives in Moose Lake, Minnesota, where he writes, translates, and directs a quiet revolution in contemporary American poetry. This reading was presented at the 1985 Humanities Seminar at Augustana College.

Some people believe that to be a writer is to engage in a moral project. I think writing has to do primarily with language — with using language precisely and accurately. And we're all involved with that project. One of the worst results of the Vietnam War was that it damaged the American language. The administration began it by insisting that their motives were noble. Do you remember that one? Johnson would always quote Lincoln when he was doing something especially despicable. Hawthorne describes in "Young Goodman Brown" people who do wicked things at night, then come back out of the woods the next day and appear in church with all the straw combed out of their hair. This double life became national policy. But if the government insists that it has no shadow at all, then the opposition will accuse them of being nothing *but* shadow.

I belonged to the left and still do, but our group wasn't any better in its use of language. For example, the left liked to call policemen "pigs." The feeling is expressed, but the sense reference is off, so it is a metaphor with one missing, or lame, leg. Our language for public discussion still has not recovered.

National debate is extremely boring now. And part of that is a lack of metaphorical precision.

Poetry has to do with paying attention to language. I'm glad to give this talk with many teachers of English in the audience. When Jean Walz spoke her introduction just now, did you notice how precise her language was? As a person who writes poetry, I take part in the traditional war against sloppiness in language. I also honor by participating in the tradition of Thoreau. Honoring that tradition, I gathered recently a collection for the Sierra Club, which will be called *The Winged Life: Selected Poetry and Prose of Thoreau.* His tradition is to observe what is around you and near you. He often said: "Why should I go to Italy when there are sections of my own county I haven't seen yet?" Not his country, but his county. That sort of witticism was really a conversation-stopper, but he meant what he said. He walked at least three hours every day, some days six, and then at home he would write, that is, work on language, for another three hours. He died at forty-four, and yet his notebooks alone make up twenty printed volumes. He achieved a staggering volume of work. His tradition is to observe what is close to you. That's not a discipline followed by many poets, but it is a discipline followed by Antonio Machado, one of the best Spanish poets of the century. Thoreau wrote his most detailed descriptions, with a corresponding magnificence of language, in prose; you'll remember his wonderful description of the battle between white and black ants in *Walden.* The poetic line he inherited could not be adopted, so to speak, to enclose detail after detail, so he wrote his observations in prose and, paradoxically, his greatest poetry lies glowing in his prose.

All of you here are interested in a third tradition: keeping the heart open to the remnants of the old mountainous Norwegian life as it is lived here in the Midwest. That heart concern is inaccurately called "ethnicity on the plains." "Ethnicity on the plains" means to me that the Norwegians won, and they allowed the Germans, and the Swedes, and the Irish to remain alive. This was very, very good of them.

If you read my first book, *Silence in the Snowy Fields,* you'll see traces of all three traditions I've mentioned, and I'll begin

10

by reciting several poems from that first book. When I was about thirty, I came back to western Minnesota, to Lac qui Parle County, and moved onto an old abandoned farm a mile or so from where I had been born, and lived there as a professional failure. I was regarded so by the town. They didn't hesitate to tell me. And actually when I think of it now, I gave them some reason. I would go into town with an old jacket I wore when writing poetry in the fields. It had survived World War II when it had been apparently hit by shrapnel. But its pockets were large enough for my notebook. I would go uptown wearing this. I felt myself to be an aristocrat, a man of leisure, you see, with my old jacket. But that is not how they felt. Years later I understood the whole thing much better when, driving a car that resembled my jacket, I heard my son say (I was taking him to the grade school): "Dad, would you let me off a block from school?"

I'll recite a poem called "Driving Toward the Lac qui Parle River." Sometimes the old Chinese poets publish a little prose passage before the poem, telling how they happened to write the poem. I like that. We say such words at poetry readings, but we're working up to printing them. Here's a few notes on this poem.

A friend who taught high school in Pine Island had decided to go with his wife to Morocco to teach, and asked me to come down to Pine Island to sell his house for him. I think he forgot to take any ads in the paper because no one ever arrived all week to look at the house. I slept on the floor for a week. I don't know if you have ever slept in a completely empty house; it is a terrifying experience. I was sure robbers would come and kill me and steal my poems. I enjoyed in this way a solid week of solitude, and then drove up to Minneapolis—west on Highway 12. The highway goes to Willmar, then to Milan, then crosses the Lac qui Parle River. Because I had been alone for a week, I heard the crickets this time, and sensed the radiant energy of the soybeans. Thoreau believed that we destroy our sensibility by talking. I hadn't talked for a week.

Driving Toward the Lac qui Parle River

I

I am driving; it is dusk; Minnesota.
The stubble field catches the last growth of sun.
The soybeans are breathing on all sides.
Old men are sitting before their houses on carseats
In the small towns, I am happy,
The moon rising above the turkey sheds.

II

The small world of the car
Plunges through the deep field of the night,
On the road from Willmar to Milan.
This solitude covered with iron
Moves through the fields of night
Penetrated by the noise of crickets.

III

Nearly to Milan, suddenly a small bridge,
And water kneeling in the moonlight.
In small towns the houses are built right on the ground;
The lamplight falls on all fours in the grass.
When I reach the river, the full moon covers it.

I had written the first two stanzas in the car, but I finally got out when I reached the Lac qui Parle River, and wrote the third stanza there. When I was done I had only five lines. The other stanzas had six. The third stanza ended as I read it:

When I reach the river, the full moon covers it.

So I waited there for a half an hour or so, because there's always the danger that if you leave the spot you will never finish the poem. I stood on the bridge for a while and finally I heard a couple of men fishing underneath the bridge—it is quite a high bridge, at Lac qui Parle—talking. Because I had been alone all week, the sound of the human voice was precious to me.

12

The last line appeared then. It's not a great line, but it finishes the poem:

A few people are talking, low, in a boat.

The next poem is called "Driving to Town Late to Mail a Letter." The poem observes a midwestern night when snow starts falling around dusk; then a wind begins. Most people stay in their houses. By the time I got to town, there was no one else in a car or walking on the streets. Nobody there and it felt so wonderful. A good thing about a snow storm also is that when you drive around for hours people think you are doing something.

Driving to Town Late to Mail a Letter
It is a cold and snowy night. The main street is deserted.
The only things moving are swirls of snow.
As I lift the mailbox door, I feel its cold iron.
There is a privacy I love in this snowy night.
Driving around, I will waste more time.

This little poem has had an unfortunate history in that it got picked up for several college anthologies and you know how that goes. Anthologists apparently are lazy and only read other anthologies, so that every other anthologist now requests this rather private poem. I told an anthologist last week: "Either choose another poem or leave me out completely. You cannot use this one." Of course I could charge $500 for this poem and that would cool them down a little bit. Usually one charges $2.00 to $3.00 a line, you know, and if I charged $500 it would cool them down. I charged $100 last month.

The next poem touches obliquely on experiences that many Norwegian immigrants had. It touches on the life of the Sjolie brothers, who lived nearby. On coming from Norway around 1890 they flipped coins and so arranged the ownership of four 160 acre farms in that section. One of the brothers, the one in this poem, got the quarter with a very large slough. He never married, perhaps because of this bad luck. When he was over sixty, he sold out, and Carol and I went to the auction. There were some touching things about it. He was a bachelor, and about to move to town. He decided to leave his dog behind. I don't know if he thought he was moving to the big life now, and he didn't want his dog, or what, but only the dog was left after the auction. The neighbors would come over and try to feed the dog later. But the dog would not take food except from his old friend. I think the dog eventually starved to death. A couple of months after the auction I woke up from a dream in the afternoon, and because I had seen the farm in the dream I drove back out there, obeying, in a way, the hint the dream gave. And this is the poem I wrote:

Afternoon Sleep
I
I was descending from the mountains of sleep.
Asleep I had gazed east over a sunny field,
And sat on the running board of an old Model A.
I awoke happy, for I dreamt of my wife,
And the loneliness hiding in grass and weeds
That lies near a man over thirty, and suddenly enters.

II
When Joe Sjolie grew tired, he sold his farm,
Even his bachelor rocker, and did not come back.
He left his dog behind in the cob shed.
The dog refused to take food from strangers.

III
I drove out to that farm when I awoke;
Alone on a hill, sheltered by trees.
The matted grass lay around the house.
When I climbed the porch, the door was open.
Inside were old abandoned books,
And instructions to Norwegian immigrants.

I saw on the floor old abandoned books, and thought, "This is what I'm going to do? Spend my life writing books which

14

people will leave behind in farm houses?" One of the books I picked up told immigrants how to write a letter in English asking for a job, and in another place urged the immigrant to be sure to keep his connection with God in his new home. I thought, this man couldn't even love a dog. How is he going to love God? That brings a little bit of the sadness of life around here. Doesn't it? A little bit of that sadness. The first version ended:

> Inside were old abandoned books
> And instructions to Norwegian immigrants to love God.

I left out the last phrase when I published it. A friend said to me, "Robert, the line is too long."

> I drove out to that farm when I awoke;
> Alone on a hill, sheltered by trees.
> The matted grass lay around the house.
> When I climbed the porch, the door was open.
> Inside were old abandoned books,
> And instructions to Norwegian immigrants.

That's the way its printed. "Instructions to Norwegian immigrants to love God" is clearer, isn't it. I think so.

I want to stay a little bit with these old Norwegian farm hands, and the way I'll do that is to read you a poem about rutabagas. In the earlier poems I recited to you, the eye observes landscape, but the eye turns now, or focuses, on an object, on the surface of an object. The French poet Francis Ponge led me to this sort of poem. I've written a poem about the orange, as we peel it, and three unfinished poems on the potato, one poem on the flounder, another on a small-sized ant heap. As far as I know there are no other poems about rutabagas. For "The Rutabaga," I adopted the form of the prose poem, which is also the form Ponge used for his object poems.

A Rutabaga

The rutabaga is such a squat, fearsome thing — a sort of German observation balloon that observes below the ground. It notices the worms pass on their thundery errands, and during the night watches weird beetles passing outside the cottage.

It is about the size of the testicle of a two-thousand pound bull. The lower half (in its double color it resembles a bobber) is pale cream, a gorgeous deep cream, the undoubtful high forehead of a man of inherited wealth. And the upper half is wine red, something urgent, a reckless furtiveness that calls attention to itself, the burglar that wears red clothes, or a hermit sitting high on a pile of rutabagas. The Burgundy color is altered here and there by whitish streaks.

In the hand it rocks in its own cool ocean world. The hand feels complimented by it, as if it had been given a gift; the solid drift of snow that keeps the henhouse warm, or the waves the storm throws against the cliff.

A knife has cut off both taproot and foliage. The cut at the bottom shows the raw flesh, as a severed head shows the neck. Faint rutabaga rings reverberate up into the skull.

When we bite into it, we taste an embittered story out of the Depression, that ends with the whole family scattered, the furniture dispersed, the old pump no longer working, a sour old man camped in the living room, and crusted cans of Carnation Condensed Milk everywhere. Last night I dreamt that Christmas was coming, and you were in the house practicing music upstairs with a young, dark-haired man . . . a drummer. Each time you hit the sheet music with your wooden stick end, notes came out. The tune was: "When the Saints Go Marching In."

So that's the poem on the rutabaga. Something strange happens sometimes when one concentrates on an object. You felt it in the end: the dream. Something strange about an object . . . the more you observe it, the deeper you get inside yourself. About three-quarters of the way through that poem, as I wrote it, I suddenly remembered a dream that I had the night before. Some people say that when one is writing a poem one is preparing a house for guests, and if one appears, he or she is to be welcomed. Sometimes one receives guests that one doesn't want, and has to ask them to leave later, but still it's important to invite them in. The dream turned out to be a thoughtful and lively guest. The dream as it is doesn't seem to make sense, but a rutabaga doesn't make sense either. I like the contrast in mood between the rutabaga and the song, "When the Saints Go Marching In." It's marvelous. I don't mean that the poem is marvelous; it's just a poem.

I'm going to move through three sections in this reading; each will take about twenty minutes. A few years after *Silence in the Snowy Fields* I put out another book called *This Tree Will Be Here For a Thousand Years.* I'll read two poems from that book. "Driving My Parents Home At Christmas" is the first. That Christmas I drove my parents over to my brother's farm, or his widow's farm, and later that night drove my parents back to their own farm. When people get old, one senses a tremendous frailty in them. I also noticed that as my parents got older they began to dwell on certain details. For example, the night before they had forgotten to take home a photograph of a grandchild from a house they had visited. When my parents were forty-five, or fifty, they would have spent twenty-five seconds on that problem. You know, have someone bring it over, or we'll pick it up. But now they returned to it again and again.

Driving My Parents Home at Christmas
As I drive my parents home through the snow,
their frailty hesitates on the edge of a mountainside.
I call over the cliff,
only snow answers.
They talk quietly

17

of hauling water, of eating an orange,
of a grandchild's photograph left behind last night.
When they open the door of their house, they disappear.
And the oak when it falls in the forest who hears it
    through miles and miles of silence?
They sit so close to each other . . . as if pressed together
    by the snow.

I'll repeat that poem, speaking it to the bouyouki this time.
You will feel the difference.

I recited poems without music for fifteen years and then became
ashamed of myself, because our ancestors always put music and
poetry together, as the *Beowulf* poets did — always there was the
harp. In southern France during the thirteenth century poets mingled poetry and music so decisively that poets, we now know,
composed the tune first, and then the poem after it. Guullaerne
IX, Bernard de Ventedorn, and Jaufre Rudel are all examples.
The tune when well composed carries them into the heart, and
that is the journey it intends. Of course it does that for me,
too. There's a danger during a poetry reading of having a cold
heart or a fearful heart.

This morning Ruth said to me, "What will it be like at the
reading tonight? Will you be scared?" I said, "I don't think so.
The audience will be mostly Norwegians and Swedes, and I understand such types." But when one is with utter strangers, the
heart may experience genuine fear and grow cold. Then the person doing the recital may find some elementary music helpful.
The first instrument I used is the American instrument called
the dulcimer, and I still use it. Lately I've adopted also this
eight-stringed instrument, a kind of Greek lute, which appears
to be an Arab lute that was brought by the Moslems to Spain
and southern France in the twelfth and thirteenth centuries. I
bought it in Athens a couple of years ago. I'll use it to recite
the next poem, "Moving Books to a New Study."

I used my chicken house, having evicted the chickens, for
years as a study. I remember that when I would go to see my
grandmother in the old people's home, she sometimes asked,
"What have you been doing, Robert?" I would answer, "I've

18

been writing as usual in the chicken house, Grandma." She would say, "Robert, couldn't you say 'study'? It sounds so much better." I would say, "Well, you know it *is* a chicken house, Grandma." "It would still sound better if you said 'study.' " After ten years or so I bought a county schoolhouse and moved it over; I think the entire schoolhouse cost me $150. One day in midwinter, after fixing it up a bit — I had originally fixed it for James and Annie Wright to use on their honeymoon earlier that year — I finally carried my favorite books over the snow to that good place, and I wrote this poem that day:

Moving Books to a New Study
First snow yesterday, and now more falling.
Each blade has its own snow balanced on it.
One mousetrack in the snow ahead,
the tailmark wavering in
between the footprints. Dusk in half an hour.

Looking up I see my parents' grove.
Somehow neither the Norwegian culture
nor the American could keep them warm.
I walk around the barn the long way
carrying the heavy green book I love through the snow.

We have to save ourselves by our own means now — the warm Norwegian culture is not going to warm us any more. American culture, as we see it on television, is becoming colder and colder. Popular American culture does not do well in keeping our people spiritually alive, especially the older people. In Norway, older people are often very much involved in the community of a single valley. They warm each other up with card parties. But in the small towns of the United States, old people are isolated one or two to a house and attached there to a cold blue light. How terrible the loneliness of each house is. Have you ever listened to the noise of television from the next room? Laughter comes every other minute. What can be so funny in this country that fully grown men and women laugh every other minute? There must be real fear. American culture does not do very well in feeding the thirsty souls of old people — or young. I'd like to stay with the Scandinavian-American heritage a little longer by talking about Bill Holm and his new book of essays. Bill writes poetry, sings, plays Bach on the harpsichord, and ragtime on the piano, teaches poetry at Southwest State, having sprung out of the soil around Minneota, Minnesota, an Icelandic colony. I'll read from his essay "The Music of Failure," which is also the title of the book:

I first heard a piano in the backroom of Peterson's farmhouse, three miles east of my father's place. An only child, too young and disinterested to do any real work, I was left indoors while my father was out giving Wilbur a hand with some chore, probably splitting a half-pint to make the job more pleasant. Wilbur was a bachelor, but kept his aged father, Steve, and a sort of combination housekeeper and nurse, Pauline Bardal, to look after both of them. Pauline was born in 1895 to the first generation of Icelandic immigrants in western Minnesota. When I knew her in the late 40's or early 50's, she must have been nearing 60. Age is relative to children, so I did not think of her as being particularly old. She was simply Pauline, and would remain that way until she died 30 years later.

She was almost six feet tall, without a bit of fat on her, and this made her bones visible, particularly in the hands, joints moving with large gestures as if each finger had reasoning power of its own. Her leanness was partly genetic, but partly also the result of continual work. In the cities she would have been called a domestic, though her duties at Peterson's and elsewhere always involved nursing the infirm and dying. . . .

After finishing her duties with bread, chickens, or tending to old Steve, Pauline retired to the den for a half hour of music. I was invited to listen and always delighted by the prospect. She sat herself on the bench, arranging her bones with great dignity and formality. Music was not a trifling matter even if your hands were fresh from

20

flour bin or hen house. Pauline did not play light music; though she was conventionally religious in a Lutheran sort of way, I knew, even as a child, that music was her true spiritual exercise. She always played slowly, and I suppose, badly, but it made no difference. She transported both herself and me by the simple act of playing. Her favorite pieces were Handel's "Largo" from *Xerxes,* and a piano arrangement of the finale of Bach's *St. Matthew Passion:* "In Deepest Grief." She had never learned true fingering, and got most of her musical experience at an old pump organ that she played for church services. She did not so much strike the keys as slide with painstaking slowness from one to the next, leaving sufficient time for the manual rearrangement of the bones in her hands. This gave all her performances a certain halting dignity, even if sometimes questionable accuracy. . . .

But Pauline at the keyboard was not a lugubrious spirit. Watching that joy on her bony face as her fingers slid over the yellowed keyboard of the old upright, it became clear to me even as a child that neither her nor my true life came from kneading bread or candling eggs or fluffing pillows in a sick bed, but happened in the presence of those noises, badly as they might be made by your own hands. They lived in the inner lines of that Bach, so difficult to manage cleanly with workstiffened fingers. . . . Even on farms in rural Minnesota, you deserve the extraordinary joy of hearing it for the first time, as if composed in your presence, only for you. I heard it that way, under Pauline's hands. The Minneapolis Symphony playing Beethoven's *Ninth* in the living room could not have been so moving or wonderful as that "Largo" in Peterson's back room. (59-60)

Bill Holm goes on to talk about the American sense of failure:

Pauline, in American terms, was a great failure: always poor, never married, living in a shabby small house when not installed in others' backrooms, worked as a domestic servant, formally uneducated, English spoken with the odd inflections of those who learn it as a second language, gawky and not physically beautiful, a badly trained musician whose performances would have caused laughter in the cities. She owned nothing valuable, traveled little, and died alone, the last of her family. If there were love affairs, no one will now know anything about them, and everyone involved is surely dead. Probably she died a virgin, the second most terrible fate, after dying broke, that can befall an American. (65)

Bill talks further about our national reluctance to acknowledge failure, which may be connected to the constant canned laughter:

Minneota is a community born out of failure about 1880. By that I mean that no one ever arrived in Minneota after being a success elsewhere. It is an immigrant town, settled by European refuse, first those starved out of Ireland, then Norway, Iceland, Sweden, Holland, Belgium. Given the harshness of western Minnesota's climate and landscape, people did not come to retire or loaf. They came to farm, and had they been successful at it in the old world, would not have uprooted their families, thrown away culture and language, and braved mosquitos and blizzards for mere pleasure. Minneota is, of course, a paradigm for the settling of the whole country. We are a nation of failures who have done all right and been lucky. Perhaps it is some ancient dark fear of repeating our own grandfathers' lives that makes us reluctant to acknowledge failure in national or private life. (65)

The last is a magnificent sentence, I think: "Perhaps it is some ancient dark fear to repeating our own grandfathers' lives that makes us reluctant to acknowledge failure in national or private life." The music of failure is the one music that Americans won't listen to. In ordinary conversation these days people present their latest disaster as a positive thing: "I had a breakdown, but it led to a lot of growth. . . . " As a nation, we refuse to go through the massive grief appropriate for the Vietnam War, which was a failure militarily, intellectually, emotionally, and politically. We hired three presidents in a row — Ford, Carter, Reagan — on their promise that they would be cheerful. We will elect anyone, even a bad actor, as long as he doesn't suggest that we've ever had a failure. This inability to hear the music of failure strikes into me because I know how difficult it's been for me to acknowledge any kind of failure in my life. The greatness of Frost lies in his ability to acknowledge personal failure, even though he wouldn't acknowledge national failure.

Perhaps this moment would be a good time to move back to our parent countries, to give a little sense of what contemporary Scandinavian poetry is like. In this section of the reading I'll alternate Scandinavian poems in translation with poems of mine. The first poem is written by Olav H. Hauge, who lives in Ulvik, Hardanger, and writes in country Norwegian, the softly pronounced language not influenced by Danish. I'll read my own translation:

Across the Swamp
It is the roots from all the trees that have died
out here, that's how you can walk
safely over the soft places.
Roots like these keep their firmness; it's possible
they've lain here centuries.
And there is still some dark remains
of them under the moss.
They are still in the world and hold
you up so you can make it over.
And when you push out into the mountain lake, high
up, you feel how the memory
of that cold person
who drowned himself here once
helps hold up your frail boat.
He, really crazy, trusted his life
to water and eternity.

23

Gorgeous, isn't it? One can feel in that poem the willingness of that older culture to go down into subjects like insanity and people drowning. There's grief there with no comfort. I'll read a second poem written by Olav H. Hauge. Country Norwegian does resemble willow branches, very delicate willow branches.

Leaf Huts and Snow Houses
These poems don't amount
to much, just
some words thrown together
at random.
And still
to me
there's something good
in making them, it's
as if I have in them for a little
while a house.
I think of playhouses
made of branches I built
as a boy:
to crawl into them, sit
listening to the rain,
in a wild place alone,
feel the drops of rain on your nose
and in your hair —
or snowhouses at Christmas,
crawl in and close it after
with a sack,
light a candle, be there
through the long chill evenings.

Lovely, isn't it? Some people believe that writing has something to do with the joy of making money, and we don't make any so we can't have much joy. But Olav Hauge says that when you write poems you are making a house for yourself where you can go in and sit. I'm much less lonely than either of my parents. And one reason is because I have worked building playhouses of leaves and snow. What is it that he says so beautiful-

24

ly? "or snowhouses at Christmas, / crawl in and close it after / with a sack, / light a candle, be there / through the long chill evenings."

I'll read a poem of mine that has something to do with failure. It is about love, but is not a victory poem. It's odd how most love poems are victories in a way. I asked myself what would a love poem be like if it wasn't about victory. I read this poem for the first time last week in California, and had to explain to them that if you leave a woollen blanket out overnight in Minnesota on the ground, the crickets will eat holes in it. This is a poem about that kind of forgetfulness:

Failing to Talk

After brooding a while over my childishness,
I notice the holes crickets have eaten in the blanket.
A man and a women stretched out asleep
Will find the cold slipping in through those holes.

What we do not want to see enters during the night,
And arriving frightens the red haired woman
Who brings her fatherly lover to the emergency door.
At the funeral people say: "How could we have missed it?"

Men and women build a shelter of blankets and live there,
And the sentences they do not speak eat at it.
What we do not care for fills the mouth
When we fail to say a certain essential word.

Written language is wonderful, and I've slowly learned that just talking is an important thing. Women know this: they often say to a man, "I wish you would talk to me more." Of course that's an unfair thing to say, because talk comes to women so much more easily than it comes to men. It is like a man saying to a woman, "Let's run the 400 today," or "Let's take the Toyota engine apart today." We have to realize that when a woman asks a man to talk to her, he has to reach way down — 10,000 miles down and back — to get those two or three words that for her just seem to bubble out of ground level. And yet women are right with their question. My family talked hardly at all, in the old Norwegian-American way. But in marriage, how important talking is. So many things we do not say need to be said. Some people, men or women, know or have learned what needs to be said. Words are proper at birthdays, certain sentences are proper at toasts, some toasts are necessary, some painful words are needed at times. When a person says something right at the right moment, everything goes well. My poem is about the absence of that proper talk.

I thought of Rolf Jacobsen a few minutes ago when I recited the poem of my own called "Driving My Parents Home at Christmas." The next poem I'll recite is by the Norwegian poet Rolf Jacobsen, who is about sixty-five now, and very much loved in Norway. He writes in city Norwegian or *bokmal*. In writing about old people he is the greatest poet I've ever known. One of the mistakes that we make about old people is believing that nothing is going on with them. Jacobsen notices this. Perhaps a grandson arrives at the house and brings a ghetto blaster along for his grandmother. She doesn't say much, and what she does say he doesn't hear. Later she remarks: "My senile grandson came to see me today." This is a poem by Rolf Jacobsen, called "Old Age":

> I put a lot of stock in the old.
> They sit looking at us and don't see us,
> and have plenty with their own,
> like fishermen along big rivers,
> motionless as a stone
> in the summer night.
>
> I put a lot of stock in fishermen along rivers
> and old people and those who appear after a
>   long illness.
> They have something in their eyes
> that you don't see much anymore
> the old, like convalescents
> whose feet are still not very sturdy under them
> and pale foreheads as if after a fever.

The old
who so gradually become themselves once more
and so gradually break up
like smoke, no one notices it, they are gone
into sleep
and light.

I'll read the end of it again. If we had time I would read everything twice. All poems should be read twice.

The old
who so gradually become themselves once more
and so gradually break up
like smoke, no one notices it, they are gone
into sleep
and light.

There's much sweetness in this poem. Have you ever seen a street lamp standing alone on the sidewalk late at night? Rolf Jacobsen, again, in my own translation:

My Street Lamp
My streetlamp is so glacially alone in the night.
The small paving stones lay their heads down
    all around
where it holds up its lightumbrella over them.
so that the wicked dark will not come near.

It says: We are all far from home.
There's no hope any more.

It's time now to recite a Swedish poet. I love the work of the contemporary Swedish poet Tomas Transtromer. He is forty-five years old or so and wields a very sharp sword. Here is a single stanza he wrote:

We got ready and showed our home.
The visitors said, "You live well.
The slum must be inside you."

It's a sharp reminder for people who live nowhere near slums. Swedish people have very few slums — on the outside.

I'll recite a poem now that Tomas Transtromer wrote on the death of Kennedy. Tomas was brought up by his mother, but an uncle was very good to him. That uncle died almost the same time as Kennedy did, and this poem, Transtromer told me, contains the shock from both those two deaths. He mentions here a suit of samurai armor in the Stockholm museum, next to which a replica of the warrior's body stands.

After a Death

Once there was a shock
that left behind a long, shimmering comet tail.
It keeps us inside. It makes the TV pictures snowy.
It settles in cold drops on the telephone wires.

One can still go slowly on skis in the winter sun
through brush where a few leaves hang on.
They resemble pages torn from old telephone directories.
Names swallowed by the cold.

It is still beautiful to feel the heart beat
but often the shadow seems more real than the body.
The samurai looks insignificant
beside his armor of black dragon scales.

I'll recite a poem next written for my father, from a book called *The Man in the Black Coat Turns*. What I could say helpfully about the poem is what is not in it. It broods about "doing what you want" — tyrants do that, some hobos, some alcoholics, some strong men and women. I have the feeling that in the small Minnesota towns more men early on did what they wanted than now. That's not all bad. They showed what their desires were, but the people around often had less of them. This poem is called "My Father's Wedding 1924." It started out as an object poem. I was examining a log or branch, writing about it, and it suddenly reminded me of my father's wounded leg, the one he hid and didn't hide. Then it looked like my leg. I had to decide if it was going to be my father's leg or mine. I decided it would be my father's, so then I wrote this poem:

My Father's Wedding 1924

Today, lonely for my father, I saw
a log, or branch,
long, bent, ragged, bark gone.
I felt lonely for my father when I saw it.
It was the log
that lay near my uncle's old milk wagon.

Some men live with an invisible limp,
stagger, or drag
a leg. Their sons are often angry.
Only recently I thought:
Doing what you want . . .
Is that like limping? Tracks of it show in sand.

Have you seen those giant bird-
men of Bhutan?
Men in bird masks, with pig noses, dancing,
teeth like a dog's, sometimes
dancing on one bad leg!
They do what they want, the dog's teeth say that!

But I grew up without dogs' teeth,
showed a whole body,
left only clear tracks in sand.
I learned to walk swiftly, easily,
no trace of a limp.
I even leaped a little. Guess where my defect is!

Then what? If a man, cautious
hides his limp,
Somebody has to limp it! Things
do it; the surroundings limp.
House walls get scars,
the car breaks down; matter, in drudgery, takes it up.

On my father's wedding day,
no one was there
to hold him. Noble loneliness
held him. Since he never asked for pity
his friends thought he
was whole. Walking alone, he could carry it.

He came in limping. It was a simple
wedding, three
or four people. The man in black,
lifting the book, called for order.
And the invisible bride
stepped forward, before his own bride.

He married the invisible bride, not his own.
In her left
breast she carried the three drops
that wound and kill. He already had
his barklike skin then,
made rough especially to repel the sympathy

he longed for, didn't need, and wouldn't accept.
They stopped. So
the words are read. The man in black
speaks the sentence. When the service
is over, I hold him
in my arms for the first time and the last.

After that he was alone
and I was alone.
No friends came; he invited none.
His two-story house he turned
into a forest,
where both he and I are the hunters.

I'll read now one last poem by Rolf Jacobsen, just to celebrate
him. He visited this country a few years ago, and we arranged
a reading tour for him to three or four Norwegian hangouts,

for example, Madison (Wisconsin), Seattle, Decorah. I read the translations for him in Madison. I had in fact translated twenty poems of his in a book accurately titled *Twenty Poems of Rolf Jacobsen*. So we read the entire book, each poem first in Norwegian, then in English. The students, most of whom knew no Norwegian, nevertheless clapped after each Norwegian version, and clapped fiercely. It was so sweet to have a good grandfather up there, and there he was: they knew the poems were sound also. Here is one of his poems that seems as if it were written for college students:

The Sunflower

What sower walked over earth,
which hands sowed
our inward seeds of fire?
They went out from his fists like rainbow curves
to frozen earth, young loam, hot sand,
they will sleep there
greedily, and drink up our lives
and explode it into pieces
for the sake of a sunflower that you haven't seen
or a thistle head or a chrysanthemum.

Let the young rain of tears come.
Let the calm hands of grief come.
It's not all as evil as you think.

Let the young rain of tears come.
Let the calm hands of grief come.
It's not all as evil as you think.

I'll recite a poem of my own now, called "A Man and a Woman and a Blackbird." In "Thirteen Ways of Looking at a Blackbird," Wallace Stevens set down these four magnificent lines:

A man and a woman
are one.
A man and a woman and a blackbird
are one.

31

If you repeat it, you'll see that it's a tune and not just words.
I took my title from his tune:

A Man and a Woman and a Blackbird
When the two rivers
join in the cloudy chamber,
so many alien nights
in our twenties, alone
on interior mountains,
forgotten. Blackbirds
walk around our feet
as if they shared
in what we know.
We know and we don't know
what the heron feels
with his wing-
tip feathers stretched
out in the air above
the flooded lake,
or the odorous constellations
the pig sees
past his wild snout.
A man and a woman
sit near each other. On
the windowpane
ice.
The man says: "How
is it
I have never loved
ice before?
If I have not loved ice,
what have I loved?
Loved the dead
in their Sumerian
fish-cloaks?
The vultures celebrating?
The soldiers
and the poor?"

And yet
for one or two
moments,
in our shared grief
and exile,
we hang our harps
on the willows,
and the willows
join us,
and the man
and the woman
and the blackbird are one.

It's getting time for a new group of poems, and this time I want to go back in Norway another eight hundred years. Why not? We'll truly get back home now. These are forty-eight-syllable poems, written around the year 1000. I thought you'd like to hear the Old Norse, so I asked Paul Schach, who is a great scholar in this field, if he would read these two poems today and he said very gallantly that he would. The texts for both poems are from Roberta Frank's *Old Norse Court Poetry*. The situation with the first poem is this. The man went to see a woman that he loved. She said to him, "My husband is waiting with some men to ambush you on the way home." He spoke this poem to her before he left. She copied down or memorized the poem when he left the house. It was preserved, and her husband and his men did kill him on their way home. The poem goes this way in my translation:

Bjorn's Farewell As He Goes into a Husband's Ambush
Our wish should be that this day, arrived
between the golden pines and the dark-
blue sea, should be the longest
day of all—woman's love is not
harmless—as now Oh young pine
tree of gold in evening twilight
I go, as I have gone so often before,
to drink the wake of my vanished joy.

You can tell that the poet is withholding some important feeling or image until the end of the poem. They build a kind of dam with their syntax, and the emotion builds up behind it. If the poet is feeling a certain sort of loneliness, you don't know that until the last line. Modern poets tend to do it differently: "I'm lonely today. How are you?" One of their greatest disciplines is to withhold. Robert Frost said, "In a poem you always hold something back."

Now listen to the way the *th's* reproduce in the original. They sound incredible. It is like a little string quartet:

Guls mundum vit vilja
viðar ok blás í miðli,
grand fæ'k af stoð stundum
strengs, þenna dag lengstan,
alls í aptan, þella,
ek tegumk sjalfr at drekka
opt horfinnar erfi,
armlinns, gleði minnar.

All right, that was beautifully read. Could you feel it? How thick it is and full of nuts and raisins? They composed on the spur, as we say, of the moment because the Norsemen of that time had memorized hundreds of these poems, with their sounds interlocking in a way similar to the necks of dragons interlocking on their church doors, and composed many while walking or riding. They did not write the poems at all; but they created them with the body. The voice, the horse-hooves, the feeling, drawing them from tremendous reservoirs of sound that the ancients prided themselves on. About to begin a poem was described as "unlocking their word-hoard." Many persons that you now hear speaking on television have only five or six words: money, great, clothes, Los Angeles. That's about it. The Old Norse had a word-hoard, so that when one bites into one of their poems it is like eating a Viennese tart, or a Napoleon. Even in the Storting, or early parliament, the poetic form was used. If someone insulted you in public, you were given maybe five minutes of silence, in which you returned the insult, or the answer, as a poem, with syllable count and repeating sounds.

I'll read it a second time now in English, using a harp I've brought with me. Tonight is a celebration for me, because I'm playing the harp for the first time in public. It is a copy of an ancient harp. The Germanic poets used a harp when reciting poetry—we know that from travel reports by Roman visitors, as well as from relief sculptures of singing poets and their harps worked into cathedral walls during the Middle Ages. They were small hand-held harps, played from the back with the left hand, and from the front with the right.

Some years ago a Viking burial mound at Sutton Hoo, England, was excavated, and though something like two thousand tons of earth had collapsed into the burial chamber, the harp buried with it had fallen, most of it, into a stone bowl, and so the pieces remained recognizable. Scholars feel absolutely confident of its size, shape, and general configuration, and the figures have been stored in the British Museum. A monk in San Francisco offered to make a copy for me, following the figures left in the British Museum, and here it is! It is identical to the original, except for the two bronze decorations, which we couldn't afford. It has eight strings. We have no idea of course what the tuning was. My wife tuned it last night in the minor scale, and that scale seems to fit this poem:

> Our wish should be that this day, arrived
> between the golden pines and the dark-
> blue sea, should be the longest
> day of all—woman's love is not
> harmless—as now Oh young pine
> tree of gold in evening twilight
> I go, as I have gone so often before,
> to drink the wake of my vanished joy.

Now let's try a second Old Norse poem. The poem was found only twenty years ago in the foundations of an old Hanseatic house on the harbor at Bergen. It had been carved on a stick, called a rune stick, and dates to about 1100. The eight lines are carved in Old Norse, and then a single line from Ovid, which finished the poem beautifully. It says, "Love conquers all, and we too give in to love." Mr. Schach, would you read this poem in the original?

Fell til friðrar þellu
fárligrar mér árla
fiskáls festibála
forn byrr hamarnorna;
þeim lundi hefr Þundar
þornlúðrs ǫlunbúðar
glaummarr gýgjartauma
galdrs fastliga haldit.

In the first four lines he says that desire for the beautiful, dangerous woman overpowered him in the old days.
I'll read it in my translation:

The Wind Blowing Off Cliffs
The ancient breeze of the cliff goddesses
fell on me early, turning me toward the handsome
dangerous young pine tree who contains
the firm fire of the fish's plains.
The hollowed out wood of the mackerel's castle
lifts a thorn; its wolf is the wind —
blowing off sea cliffs — holding fast
the man who is a bush of Odin's magical tree.
OMNIA VINCIT AMOR: ET NOS CEDAMUS AMORI

You have to know that for them to call a ship a ship was deeply boring; who would ever do that? Would you call an ocean an ocean? At least it's "the whale's home." I've left my translation a little awkward so you can hear some of the fun the composer is having with nouns, and the listeners feel the fun also. A girl is not a girl but a "young pine tree of gold." You heard that in the ambush poem. That allows the shape and the freshness and the divine quality of a woman to be brought together into

36

a single image. The word *woman* is not sufficient to describe a woman. It's wrong to call a woman a woman. "Young pine tree" and "gold" evoke feelings and thoughts that are evoked by the actual woman.

When we first hear such elaborate locutions, the authors seem to be practicing a conspicuous consumption of language. Actually they are trying to be truly accurate. In this last poem, a woman is described as wind coming off sea cliffs. As boatmen, they went past a lot of cliffs. And every time the wind came up they knew it was a woman. Sometimes a dangerous one too. What is a ship? An ocean can be "the whale's road" or the "whale's home," and, if so, it can surely be "the mackerel's castle." Isn't that right? Then a ship is the hollowed out wood of the mackerel's castle. That's certainly true.

Reading Old Norse poems is like opening a Chinese box, with other red and gold lacquered boxes inside. The ocean is the mackerel's castle. The hollowed out wood of the mackerel's castle is a ship. The mast of the ship is a thorn. And what is the wolf of the mast? Wind. If you were an old Norse poet, you wouldn't just say "wind," would you? How disgusting. What's the weather today? The wolf of the mast is running forty miles an hour. That makes daily life more interesting. As for the man who writes poetry, he is "the bush of Odin's magical tree." What's your work? "I'm the bush of Odin's magical tree."

So he identifies himself as a religious man at the very last line. But he says his religious nature isn't going to do any good because this wind coming off the sea cliffs is too strong. I know what he means. I think you do too.

The sea cliffs, the wind, the wolf, the man held fast by magical air suggest many other thoughts that are a part of the poem, just as much as the ones I've mentioned. I'll read it once more in English:

The ancient breeze of the cliff goddesses
fell on me early, turning me toward the handsome
dangerous young pine tree who contains
the firm fire of the fish's plains.
The hollowed out wood of the mackerel's castle

lifts a thorn; its wolf is the wind—
blowing off sea cliffs—holding fast
the man who is a bush of Odin's magical tree.
OMNIA VINCIT AMOR: ET NOS CEDAMUS AMORI

I'll recite two more poems of mine as a way of closing. The
first poem is an eighty-five-syllable form which I invented, so
to speak, myself, and named "the ramage." Writing the first
of them six or seven years ago, and then later, reading Roberta
Frank's book, I found to my surprise that my ancestors had
worked, as in the poems above, for centuries in a forty-eight-
syllable form, also divided into eight lines. We're a little more
talkative anyway, I suppose, as Americans. I'll recite then a ramage
called "The Ancient Man":

What choice do we have but to go down? How can I
be close to you if I am not sad? The clam
tumbles in the surf, and amber holds the secret desires
the bee felt before his room grew silent.
The lonely man reads by his lamp at night.
What is it that we want? Some ancient man, half-
bear, and half-human, knows what we want.
The more he talks to us, the swifter we tumble down.

A woman hearing the poem could say the lines this way:

Some ancient woman, half-
bear, and half-human, knows what we want.

It doesn't do any harm to rewrite a poem. The poem belongs
to the speaker.
I'll finish with a poem called "The Good Silence":

Reading an Anglo-Saxon love poem in its
    extravagance,
I stand up and walk about the room.
I do not love you in a little way;
oh yes, I do love you in a little way,

38

the old way, the way of the rowboat alone in
    the ocean.

The image is a white-washed house, on David's Head,
    in Wales,
surrounded by flowers, bordered by seashells
and withies. A horse appears at the door
minutes before a storm; the house stands
in a space awakened by salt wind, alone on its cliff.

I take your hand as we work, neither of us speaking.
This is the old union of man and woman,
nothing extraordinary; they both feel a deep
calm in the bones. It is ordinary affection
that our bodies experienced for ten thousand years.

During those years we stroked the hair of the old,
    brought in
roots, painted prayers, slept, laid hair
on fire, took lives, and the bones
of the dead gleamed from under rocks where the love
the roaming tribe gave them made them shine
    at night.

And we did what we did, made love attentively, then
dove into the river, and our bodies joined as calmly
as the swimmer's shoulders glisten at dawn,
as the pine tree stands in the rain at the edge of
    the village.
The affection rose on a slope century after century,

And one day my faithfulness to you was born.
We sit together silently at the break of day.
We sit an hour, then tears run down my face.
"What is the matter?" you say, looking over.
I answer, "The ship saileth on the salte foam."

WORKS CITED

Frank, Roberta. *Old Norse Court Poetry*. Ithaca, N.Y.: Cornell UP, 1978.

Holm, Bill. *The Music of Failure*. Marshall, Minn.: Plains, 1985.

The Slip-Up Settlement and Ole Rölvaag

CLARENCE BERDAHL

Clarence Berdahl is professor emeritus of politcal science at the University of Illinois and the brother of Ole Rölvaag's wife, Jennie. This paper was presented at the 1984 Berdahl-Rölvaag Lecture Series.

The Slip-Up saga begins in Norway about the middle of the eighteenth century. In 1780 a family by the name of Hamre came from Sjöstrand (now Leikanger), on the north side of Sognefjord, and settled on some acres near the village of Feios, on the opposite side of the fjord. That farm, about a mile up the mountain from Feios, overlooking Sognefjord, was next to a deep and fertile valley where berries flourished, hence the name Berdahl (valley of berries), which then became the family name. In 1974, almost two hundred years later, I picked raspberries there for a week, that being then their commercial crop.

However, those who became the Slip-Up Settlement did not come directly from Berdahl. My grandfather, Johannes Berdahl, was the second son and, therefore, under Norway's law (Odelstret), could not inherit any portion of Berdahlsgard. He had married Kristi Henjum from across the fjord. They had to make a living, and moved to Jordal, roughly about ten miles from Berdahl, midway on Fjärlandsfjord, a branch of Sognefjord running about ten miles north from the well-known resort Balholm or Balestrand, and ending at Mundal, a tiny village from which former Vice-President Walter Mondale's grandfather emigrated to the United

States. Jordal, by contrast to Berdahl, was and still is a small gard, located between the fjord and a high and steep mountain, and has almost no level ground. It was literally a place easy to fall off of into the sea, and one of the young boys (Uncle Anfin) did exactly that and had to be fished out of deep water, while another (Uncle Erick) fell onto a rock on the water's edge, getting a scar on his nose and forehead that remained throughout his life. In that area the mountains came down so near the water's edge that there was no room for roads and the only way to get to the village or to church or anywhere was by boat. That was the situation when Sister Ida and I visited Jordal in 1925. The old lady who kept us overnight rowed us into the middle of the fjord so we could see the glacier at Mundal and climb on board the steamer that took us back to Balholm. There in Jordal, Grandfather was *Husman* or renter; there four children were born (three boys and one girl, my father Anders, which became Andrew, the oldest); there they somehow survived for eight years (1848-1856), and had they remained there I suppose our name would have been Jordal instead of Berdahl.

But the living was hard, with almost no cash return, and probably occasionally short rations, for I understand that they were sometimes even eating bark bread, bread made from ground-up bark with just a little flour; so they were easily persuaded to emigrate to America, which was already being talked about as a land of promise and to which two or three young men from the Feios area had recently gone. Moreover, a well-to-do farmer (Peder Wilson Rödbotten), who was himself about to emigrate, offered to lend the money for the voyage, $120 for the entire family; this, as my father described the transaction, "without the scratch of a pen," just on Father's oral promise that he would pay it to him as soon as he could make it (which he did by installments over a period of five or six years). That amount, which must seem to us impossibly trivial for a family of six, covered only transportation; the passengers provided their own food, so some time had to be spent in preparation for the voyage. But they sailed in May 1856, by "freight schooner" from Jordal and Berdahl to Bergen and by an old sailing ship, *Columbus,* from Bergen to Quebec, a voyage of eight weeks and two days. From Quebec they sailed up the St. Lawrence River to Montreal, through the Great Lakes to Chicago; from Chicago they rode the Illinois Central Railroad, then just completed, to Galena, Illinois, on the Mississippi River, and from Galena by river boat to Lansing, Iowa, a river town in the northeast corner of that state. There they found two Norwegians who drove them and their baggage by ox teams and lumber wagons the fifty miles to the Big Canoe settlement in Winneshiek County, where Grandfather Berdahl had a distant relative and which was the family's immediate destination. They reached this after twelve weeks of arduous travel, and my father no doubt expressed the family's feelings when he wrote many years later, "I can remember how good Mrs. Fretheim's food tasted after subsisting for three months on the food prepared in Norway."

In this area the family lived four years, moving from farm to farm as opportunities occurred for work or rent, but gradually improving their lot and always sending the boys to school, whatever the walking distance, usually three or four miles. In the spring of 1860 they moved across the state line into Houston County, Minnesota, near Spring Grove, a community almost solidly Norwegian and including an Otterness family from which my mother came. There they lived for seven years (until 1867), when they moved once more, this time a few miles west into Fillmore County, also heavily Norwegian, where they, in a sense, settled down and even began to prosper. Their Americanization was perhaps hastened by the Civil War, Grandfather casting his first vote for Lincoln in 1860, and Father, too young for the draft, joining a military company organized under a government order to train older men and young boys for future service.

Although the family was now well adjusted and living quite comfortably, it had also increased to eleven, nine children (seven boys and two girls), and more land was badly needed. They knew about the Homestead Act passed during the Lincoln Administration; they learned that free land was still available in Dakota Territory, so in May 1872, five men, including Grandfather, Father, and Uncle Erick, drove by two horse-teams and covered wagons to Sioux Falls, hired a surveyor (Cyrus Walts) to show them around, and came finally to the Slip-Up Creek.

At that time Slip-Up Creek was a good flowing stream. The scouting party was well pleased, each one picked his claim, and they traveled the sixty miles to Vermillion, then the land office, to make their filings. They returned to the Slip-Up area, where Father and Uncle Erick broke about five acres of the virgin prairie on each of the five claims (this being required to hold the land) and helped to build a sod-house for one of the five (Lasse Bothun), who moved his family there that fall.

Altogether, that first trip to Dakota Territory took about five or six weeks, but the same three (Grandfather, Father, and Uncle Erick) made a second trip that fall in order to fulfill the requirements of the Homestead Act, to live on the land within six months and to make some improvements. They could not leave until after the November election because they had to vote for Grant. They had had exceptionally pleasant fall weather in Minnesota, and went lightly dressed, encountered two severe blizzards, one each way, one of their horses died from exhaustion on the way home, and they themselves came through only because they were lucky enough to suffer these disasters near habitation and to receive generous assistance. They managed to satisfy the legal requirements by sleeping on the land a couple of nights and by building a small lean-to out of trees or branches brought from along the Sioux River four miles away.

Preparations for the final move began immediately, and about the middle of May 1873, a caravan of ten covered wagons assembled at Calmar, Iowa, and started for Slip-Up, later joined on the way by one more. Six of the covered wagons were drawn by horse-teams, five by ox-teams who, of course, set the pace. They carried eight different families, most related or from the same area in Norway, but including two Protestant Irish families (Powers) and one Catholic Irishman (Mike Tobin), who happened on the caravan and was invited to join. Together these families were followed by a herd of eighty-five cattle, thirty sheep, and eight colts, giving the young boys excitement and work to keep these animals rounded up and following the wagons. Grandfather went ahead of the caravan in order to have a sod-house ready for the family on arrival; so my father, who had made the two previous trips and knew the way, became the leader of the caravan. There were numerous problems and difficulties on the way, but the expedition reached the Slip-Up Creek on 18 June, after a month's travel, and thus began the Slip-Up Settlement. Its centennial was celebrated in Sioux Falls and in the Slip-Up area for three days in 1973.

Grandfather died in 1883, at sixty-one, after ten years in the settlement, and Uncle John died two years later (1885) of sunstroke. But within a few years, each of the six remaining Berdahl brothers had his own farm, four touching the Slip-Up, five touching one another, only one (Uncle Anfin) settling about four miles from the Slip-Up, probably because he was too young to file with the first. He soon left that farm to become a merchant in Garretson. One other family, that of Lasse Bothun, who was in fact the real pioneer in this region, also settled on the Slip-Up and became a full-fledged member of the Berdahl group through the marriage of Uncle Ole to his daughter, our Aunt Lizzie. In other words, the Slip-Up Settlement came to be a compact community of fifty persons, closely related, intermingling frequently, working and playing together. In our own case, Father and Uncle Herman, who inherited Grandfather's homestead, had married Otterness sisters. Our houses were only a few rods apart, we had a common pasture, shared some farm implements, and we lived almost as one family. The sod-houses were soon replaced, some at first by log cabins and then by bigger and fancier houses, ours by the house you see on the Augustana campus. The treeless prairie was transformed by groves and some heavily wooded areas on every farm.

Schools were organized almost at once, District No. 13 being established in its own sod-house the next year after the caravan's arrival, with my father as its teacher for the first few years. A church congregation, Norway Lutheran Church, was also organized in the spring of 1874, but the church was built five miles from Slip-Up, a fact that made church attendance often difficult in the winter months. I am sure I do not need to remind this audience of the factional divisions of the Norwegian Lutherans which by my time had been resolved into three major groups, the Norwegian Synod on the right, Hauge's Synod on the left, and Forende Kirke (the United Norwegian Lutheran Church) in the center. We belonged to the United Church, but the road we generally traveled took us by the Norwegian Synod Church, on the spot where the EROS Data Center is now located and only three miles from home. We frequently met the pastor and members of the Synod's congregation who passed by our church on the way to their own church. I sometimes wondered why those additional miles were necessary.

Four Irish Catholic families—the Donovans, the Finnegans, the McBrides, and the McKittricks—settled on our western fringe. We went to school together, attended one another's weddings and funerals, and had the best of neighborly relations. Annie Donovan learned to speak Norwegian, especially the Trondheim dialect, married a Norwegian Lutheran boy, and became a Lutheran; another Norwegian Lutheran boy married Mary McKittrick and became a Catholic, so the odds were even.

The Slip-Up Settlement always had long distances to market. The nearest railroad station was at first Worthington, sixty miles away, then Luverne and Beaver Creek, and finally Garretson, Baltic, and Renner, each an equidistant eight miles, a tough distance for winter hauling of grain or hogs, but a distance Cousin Julian and I enjoyed, driving cattle to the Garretson stockyards.

Living was hard but never dull. A debating society was organized the first Slip-Up winter (December 1873) and met in Father's sod-house; and later a house of representatives met in District No. 13 school house, debated and passed bills which were signed or vetoed by an acting president. In my time, the church choir met for choir practice every Saturday evening at one of the Berdahl homes, but that also became a social evening for everybody in the neighborhood. The Edison Concert Band was organized with a professional conductor from Sioux Falls, and performed at Early Settlers' picnics, Fourth of July celebrations, political meetings, and even in churches, playing some of the best-known hymns transposed for band by our conductor, Mr. Stevens. Christmas was celebrated over most of the twelve days by parties at the several homes and "going Julebuk" (Christmas ghosts), that is, dressing up in clownish costumes, masking, and driving around by bobsled or lumber wagon to the neighbors, at each of which there would be coffee and refreshments. Even harvesting

46

and threshing became enjoyable events in that the families assisted one another and turned the hard work into social occasions.

Father had many interests other than farming, took an active part in government and politics, and consequently was, by himself or with the family, away from the farm on several occasions, for longer and shorter periods. He was a merchant for about eight years, five years in Baltic with John O. Langness (1887-1892) and almost three years in Garretson with his brother, Uncle Anfin (1893-1896), moving back to the farm in the spring of 1896. Before that he had held several government offices, which took much of his time and paid very little: coroner and acting sheriff, sheriff and county assessor; township assessor for probably twenty years; county commissioner (1893-1896), that during the period of the drought and the hiring of a rainmaker. Father was almost mobbed because he opposed the rainmaker. He had something to do with the division of Dakota Territory into two states, and was a delegate to the Constitutional Conventions of 1885 and 1889 that wrote the Constitution of South Dakota. When the Populists carried Minnehaha County in 1896 and elected Father's Baltic partner (John O. Langness) as county treasurer, he served as a clerk in that office for two years. He left the farm permanently after Mother's death in 1915 and served the rest of his life in the county auditor's office.

But it was through Father's interest in education and his special interest in Augustana College that Ole Rölvaag came into the Slip-Up family. Augustana began in Chicago as a Norwegian-Swedish college, with the name Augustana Seminary; it was moved to Paxton, Illinois, about twenty-five miles from my University of Illinois, and was so Scandinavian a community that our *Heimskringla* would meet there for its festive celebrations. From Paxton, the Norwegian part of Augustana was moved to Marshall, Wisconsin, and there Father attended it for a winter term in 1869, passing by the much better known Luther College, which was nearer. The Swedes had meantime moved to Rock Island, Illinois, where the Swedish Augustana College has been ever since. Later on the Norwegians moved again, first to Beloit, Iowa, and then directly across the Big Sioux River to Canton, South Dakota, where the college remained until a later church union

47

provided the impetus for the move to Sioux Falls to unite with the Synod's Lutheran Normal School and become the Augustana College we now have. Brother John served Augustana as teacher and registrar in both Canton and Sioux Falls.

Father became a member of the Augustana Board in 1900, and secretary-treasurer of a building committee organized the next year to move the one building from downtown to a new site and to add a new building. That seemed to mean that Father was in charge of the construction, so the family moved to Canton and lived there for two years (1901-1903), until the building was completed and ready for students. I learned only recently that there was no general contractor and that Father's supervision meant not only keeping the books but actually hiring and paying the workmen, watching the construction, even doing some of the work himself. For those two years in Canton Father received $800, donating one year's pay to the college. The family moved back to the farm in the spring of 1903, as Father put it, "poorer financially but richer in experience, and in the knowledge that we had been helping to build a better school."

All this meant that Augustana College, only an academy though called a college, became *the* school for the Berdahls; virtually all of us who grew up in the Slip-Up Settlement and nearby attended Augustana in Canton, and it was there that we became acquainted with Ole Rölvaag. He had come, as a young man twenty years old, to the Elk Point area in 1896, and worked for two years with his uncle as a farm hand in that neighborhood. The story of those two years is best told in his book *Amerika Breve (Letters from America),* the first of his books to be published, but the last to be translated, the translation done in 1971 by his daughter Ella Valborg Tweet and his granddaughter Solveig Zempel under the title *The Third Life of Per Smevik.* After those two years, Ole Rölvaag enrolled at Augustana College and during his three years there became closely associated with several of our family, including Sister Jennie, whom he later married. He made several visits to our farm, and there I heard my father tell him about the migration to Dakota Territory, about the grasshoppers, the heavy snow winters, and other pioneer experiences that became the features of his great novel *Giants in the Earth.* He married Sister Jennie 9 July 1908, the wedding ceremony in Norway Church and the reception on our farm, a wedding I remember very well because I turned the ice cream freezer all afternoon. I did have the special privilege of living close to him during my years at St. Olaf College, first in the dormitory of which he was proctor, and Jennie with him, then in the house he built on Manitou Street, where he wrote his books. I married Evelyn Tripp, of a pioneer Yankton family, out of the English faculty at the University of Illinois. Norwegian was to her a strange language, but she had what to her was a most exciting experience of working with Ole Rölvaag, polishing the rough translations into appropriate English. She spent the entire summer of 1929 with the Rölvaag family in Northfield, and he came to Urbana and lived with us during the month of May 1931, in order that they could work together before we left for fifteen months in Europe. He died that November, while we were abroad.

The Slip-Up Settlement, as we knew it, is no more, the last acre of a Berdahl farm having changed hands four years ago. But Ole Rölvaag's family, now in the second and third generation, is not only distinguished in education, scholarship, politics, public service, and business, but continues to make major contributions to the maintenance of our Norwegian heritage. I am proud to have been somehow associated with what is represented by the Berdahl-Rölvaag House.

The Pioneer Heroine as Idea:
South Dakota's Women Writers, 1940-1970

RUTH ANN ALEXANDER

Ruth Ann Alexander is head of the English department at South Dakota State University. She delivered this paper at the 1985 Berdahl-Rölvaag Lecture Series.

The western frontier has been meaningful in American culture not only as fact but also as idea. Historians have recorded its influence upon our political, economic, and social development in fact and theory. But it is also significant to us for what it symbolizes, for its impact upon our imaginations. If we wish to *experience* some human endeavor, to understand it not just with our minds, but in our hearts and souls as well, we turn not to history, but to art — frequently to the novelist and the poet. Literary art gives shape and form and meaning to the facts. Thus, Mark Twain makes vivid and real the experience of growing up on the Mississippi River; William Faulkner brings to life a genuine southern community in Yoknapatawpha County. In Hawthorne's *Scarlet Letter* we enter the seventeenth century Puritan world of Boston; and Ole Rölvaag creates the quintessential Norwegian pioneer in Per Hansa in *Giants in the Earth*.

Yet to what literature do we turn if we wish to understand western settlement as the women who participated in it understood it? Who imagines the pioneer women into being? Who gives shape and form to her experience? Distinguished writers of the region — Rölvaag, Hamlin Garland and Frederick Manfred — have drawn literary portraits of women, sometimes vividly. For many readers, the figure of Beret in *Giants in the Earth* has come to symbolize the pioneer woman — reluctantly accompanying her husband into the wilderness, obsessed by fear of the open space of the prairie, driven beyond the limits of sanity by her own guilt. Yet at the end of the novel, Beret is the strong survivor and in two later, less popular novels of the trilogy, *Peder Victorious* and *Their Father's God,* her strength matures and mellows. Garland's woman in *Main-Travelled Roads* is often shown as a joyless drudge, isolated from cultural and social nourishment, maintaining a pioneer household in primitive conditions, enduring endless days of cooking, cleaning, washing. She, too, is a victim. Manfred's best-known work focuses on male characters with women assigned traditional roles as sexual partners, lovers, wives of Hugh Glass, Conquering Horse, Maury Grant. Women's activitives in his work seem peripheral to the main drama of western settlement.

These pictures do not tell the whole story — they are incomplete. They do not emcompass the reality created by women writers who chronicled the lives of women pioneers from the viewpoint of those who experienced homesteading, early ranching, or living in a raw, new prairie town. The shape and form of women's lives on the prairie frontier that emerges in their stories is very different from that of the male writers. Women dominate the pages of their work.

Such women writers often create a "heroine" — a woman who has great demands placed upon her by her environment. Pioneer life requires physical courage, ingenuity, self-reliance, and independence — traits more often associated with heroes than with heroines, yet qualities she demonstrates. She is usually a young woman who grows, learns, thinks, and acts. She does not see herself as a "reluctant pioneer" victim, a drudge or a sex object — in fact, she loves the freedom that life on the land or in a pioneer community gives her. She finds the wide expanse of prairie and sky, the sweeping winds, the awesome beauty of mountains and badlands, the violent cycle of weather from blizzard, tornado, and drought to lush spring mornings and luxuriant autumn afternoons a challenge to which she can whole-heartedly respond. Her adventures frequently grow out of the nature of the land and the settlements in the early years.

Between 1890 and 1970, South Dakota produced more than a score of books written by women who retold the story of the pioneer heroine again and again. The upper midwest — Minnesota, Iowa, Nebraska, North Dakota — produced others as well. They range from the famous Bess Streeter Aldrich to the popular Laura Ingalls Wilder to the unknown Stella Gilman to the forgotten Martha Ostenso. The best known woman writer of this material is, of course, Willa Cather. In Alexandra Bergson of *O Pioneers!* and in Ántonia Shimerda of *My Ántonia,* Cather has not only created strong pioneer heroines who flourish and bloom when planted on the Nebraska prairie, but she has lifted the subject to the level of genuine art.

These heroines are veritable earth mothers, identifying with the land, bringing it and themselves to fruition. In *O Pioneers!,* published in 1913, Alexandra comes to the "Wild Land" of the south central Nebraska prairies with her Swedish family. Her father recognizes her strength of will and love of the land and leaves her in charge of the homestead when he dies. His confidence is not misplaced, because during the hard years, she does not give in to her brothers who want to leave but is determined to hold on to the land. She is a strong, matriarchal figure who succeeds as a pioneer, making decisions, planning the future, building a large successful farm out of the homestead. In no sense is she a "reluctant pioneer" or a "victim" or a "drudge."

Yet Willa Cather was curiously detached from her heroines, and in most of her work evokes a nostalgic elegy for pioneer days of the past. She *observes* her pioneer heroines — she does not identify with them. In *My Ántonia,* the narrator is a male, Jim Burden, who tells the story of Ántonia — who admires and loves, but does not share, her attachment to the land. Cather herself left Nebraska and also wrote about the stifling atmosphere and the cultural emptiness of small midwestern towns. If she wrote about herself, it was in *Song of the Lark,* where Thea escapes the artistic aridity of her western birthplace to become an opera singer, in much the same way that Cather escaped to become a novelist.

In this respect, she differs from most of the women writers who drew spiritual and personal nourishment *as women* from the pioneer experience. Willa Cather was a literary artist who used the material to express her ideas and to create a usable past for the imagination. Most of the women writers of South Dakota wrote their stories to express themselves, to assert their own being and sense of self in a world which might not otherwise recognize them as important. They usually based their stories on their own experience or that of mothers, grandmothers, great-grandmothers. Some of them were professional writers, but many did not start to write until they were middle-aged or older—after they had reared a family, taught a school, become a librarian, or a newspaper reporter. Most of them were not feminists in the sense that they worked actively for women's suffrage or women's rights. Nor did they think of themselves as literary artists. They frequently wrote for the young reader; hence their heroines were often young girls growing up on the prairie.

All of them felt compelled to tell the story—a liberating story—of a young woman's discovery of herself in the leveling atmosphere of a Dakota frontier setting. The pioneer heroines that these writers created flourished on a homestead, on a ranch, or in a new prairie town. Even though she might find herself in conflict with traditional demands that she conform to an accepted standard of behavior, she engaged in activities that would be denied to her altogether in more settled communities—exploring the open prairie, riding stride, working out of doors, sharing male activities, taking responsibility, making decisions. She was not confined to domestic work according to the so-called "cult of true womanhood"—which had dominated nineteenth-century American culture.[1] Such a notion of "true womanhood" carefully delineated male and female "spheres" of activity and glorified the woman in the home—innocent, pious, submissive, domestic, white-skinned, delicate in health and sensibilities and inclined to blush, faint and weep frequently. Such qualities the pioneer heroine disdained!

Although a wealth of critical material has appeared evaluating Willa Cather's work, little critical attention has been paid to the work of these South Dakota women writers. They focus intensely upon the saga of a young woman coming to a sense of her own maturity — either as an adolescent growing up or as a young wife struggling to make a home on the prairie. They draw upon a traditional theme in American literature — the initiation into adulthood of the central character, in this case female rather than male. Their stories recount the pioneer heroine's maturation — physically, emotionally, and spiritually — in a prairie setting.

South Dakota women writers can be grouped into three historical periods. The first generation wrote their work from the time of statehood to World War I and were, therefore, close to the time of settlement. Most of them wrote directly from experience — as members of families who had migrated from eastern or middle western states, tracing their heritage to New York, Pennsylvania, or New England, in the classic pattern of settlement. Noticeably absent in this first generation of writers are women of Scandinavian or other ethnic background. Their work would not appear until considerably later. Nor are Indian women writers included. Although Zitkala-Ša (Gertrude Bonnin), a Yankton woman, published a good deal during these years, she did not turn naturally to the novel — a European literary form — but to old Indian legends and stories from her childhood.[2] Indian women did not depart from their oral traditions of literature until much later in the century.

Out of the imaginations and the sometimes awkward and clumsy literary efforts of this first generation of women writers emerges the image of the pioneer heroine. Such writers still cherished such values of the east as culture, education, and religion (not always easy to practice in raw pioneer communities) — but they whole-heartedly embraced the physical and psychological freedom of western life. They created an image of a young woman whose gentility, piety, and refinement were rooted in eastern values, but whose courage, physical energy, and independence were drawn from life on the prairie.

54

Good examples of the early pioneer heroine can be found in Nitelle M'Jarrow, the improbably named heroine in Stella Gilman's *That Dakota Girl* (1900); in the "little girl" in Eleanor Gates' *Biography of a Prairie Girl* (1902) and *The Plow Woman* (1904); in Mary Williston in Kate and Virgil Boyles' *Langford of the Three Bars* (1907). These young women reveled in the western experience.

The first heroine, Nitelle M'Jarrow, speaks "boarding school French" on a Sioux River ranch, but also whistles, shoots, hunts, fishes, plays practical jokes, and is outrageously independent in her behavior. She beats her eastern lover in a horse race, rescues him in a blizzard, and puts on a shooting demonstration worthy of Natty Bumppo in the Leatherstocking Tales, killing two birds with one shot. Other heroines, Eleanor Gates' women, homestead near the Vermillion and Missouri Rivers. The "little girl" in the *Biography* herds cattle, hunts gophers, breaks a pony, and races from a prairie fire in a series of exciting adventures growing up. Dallas in *The Plow Woman* breaks sod to provide a home for her crippled father and sister. We see her working in a slouch hat, wiping her face on the sleeve of her jersey, hitching her skirt through her waistband to "cool her ankles," plowing in a red flannel petticoat. And she enjoys it! She saves the family in a winter storm, risks her life for her sister, and faces up bravely to claim jumpers, outlaws, hostile Indians, and wild animals. A third heroine, Mary Williston in *Langford,* also defends her home, firing shot for shot with her father. She cares for the horses and does the work of a "boy" on the ranch.[3]

The second generation of writers published their work between World War I and World War II. This group caused the pioneer heroine to blossom into a genuine literary creation. More than a dozen women wrote novels or stories about young women growing up, having adventures, and making lives in pioneer South Dakota. Among them are the best known, Laura Ingalls Wilder and her daughter Rose Wilder Lane. Others, Lucile Fargo, Ethel Hueston, Edith Eudora Kohl, Marian Hurd McNeeley, and Frances Gilchrist Wood are also worthy of mention. Such writers were more polished and skillful in their craft than the first generation, and they appealed to a much larger group of readers. They were much farther removed in time from pioneer life; indeed, many of them wrote during middle-age or later. Possibly for this reason, they were able to sharpen and heighten the image of the pioneer heroine, to develop a more fully realized portrait. Their heroines were more conscious of feminist ideas.

Some representative but less well-known examples of the heroines created by these writers are Becky Linville, homesteading as a young girl with her brother near Dallas, South Dakota, in Marian Hurd McNeeley's *The Jumping Off Place* (1929); Janet Craig, a young wife homesteading near Blunt in Frances Gilchrist Wood's *Turkey Red* (1938); and Lucile Fargo's *Prairie Girl* (1937) and *Prairie Chautauqua* (1943).[4] The first heroine, Becky, holds her family together through a summer drought, teaches school so that they can survive the winter, and triumphs in that classic pioneer experience of the pioneer heroine—saving a school house full of children during a blizzard. Janet Craig, the second heroine, also triumphs, in her case saving a whole town by single-handedly getting out the paper she and her husband print. At one point in the novel, she changes roles with her husband when he has injured his hand so seriously that he cannot haul freight to Huron. Janet joyfully does his job while he, with reluctance and disdain, stays on the homestead to do her work and take care of their small son. He is not very successful, but he learns respect for "women's work" in the process.

The third heroine, "Prairie Clark" in *Prairie Girl* and *Prairie Chautauqua,* has all sorts of adventures growing up in Dell Rapids in the 1880s, including a debate in school with her friend Wells over the issue of women's rights. She becomes a teacher and also saves children during a blizzard. In the second volume, she rides her bicycle to Lake Madison for three weeks of camping with a friend in Chautauqua.

These stories were written long after the events in them occurred. The first generation of writers had written directly from their experience. These heroines asserted their presence in a land which appeared inhospitable to women. The writers described heroines who not only survived but thrived in an environment which required strength, courage, resourcefulness, and self-reliance. The second generation returned in their imaginations to the past to recreate the experience of young adulthood. Here they had discovered their true selves. Like the first heroines, their young women triumphed in the challenge of living in Dakota. They represented the ideal of the free and independent female spirit nurtured on the plains and prairie.

By the 1940s and World War II, pioneer days were half a century in the past. Yet the story which had so captured the imagination of the earlier women continued to exert its power over a new generation of writers. In the years following World War II, some nine writers turned to South Dakota's past for inspiration in creating pioneer heroines, with greater or lesser success. Yet the writing does not follow the pattern of earlier efforts exactly, but demonstrates some departures in handling the subject. In the third generation of writers, for instance, ethnic diversity and ethnic conflict play a major role in the stories.

Other earlier writers had, of course, mentioned cultural diversity. The acculturation of the Norwegian immigrant and conflict with other ethnic groups, notably the Irish, constitutes a large part of Ole Rölvaag's work. Willa Cather was also intensely interested in the clash of European culture on the Nebraska frontier in *O Pioneers!* and *My Ántonia.* Even Hamlin Garland touched upon it in his story "Among the Corn Rows." Julie Peterson has to plow the fields for her father, although she longs to persuade her parents to follow more American ways. She dreams of a romantic hero who will take her away from her stern father: "He would be a Yankee, not a Norwegian; the Yankee didn't ask their wives to work in the field. Perhaps he'll live in town — perhaps a merchant" (Garland 109). Similarly, for the first and second generations of South Dakota women writers (Stella Gilman, Eleanor Gates, Sarah Brush, for example), the Norwegian or the Indian emerged only as an inferior, or as a servant — perhaps reflecting the Yankee background of the writers.

By the mid-twentieth century, Scandinavian women writers — daughters and granddaughters of immigrants — appear to write about South Dakota pioneer life: Borghild Dahl, Inga Hansen Dickerson, Doris Stensland. In addition, the combination of mother and daughter who wrote together under the name of Mary Worthy Breneman addressed the settlement of German-Russian immigrants in *The Land They Possessed* (1956). Possibly these descendants of immigrants felt comfortable enough with English to use it to create stories of their ethnic roots. Despite the ethnic diversity, these writers also emphasize a central female character.

Borghild Dahl is particularly illustrative of this new development in pioneer stories of women. A second generation Norwegian, Borghild Dahl was born in Minneapolis in 1890 where her parents had settled after emigrating from Norway. Fiercely ambitious for education, she graduated from the University of Minnesota, did graduate study at Oslo and Columbia Universities, and became a teacher. From 1926 to 1939, she lived in South Dakota, teaching English at Augustana College and delivering a weekly book review on a local radio station. She later won the Augustana Regents Medal in 1975. In 1941, she stopped teaching because of blindness, which resulted from vision problems she had struggled with all her life. At that point, in middle age, she began to write. Her best known book, the autobiographical *I Wanted to See,* was a best seller in 1944 as an inspiration to returning service men blind from World War II. Thereafter, she turned to the subject which had absorbed so many earlier writers. Her very next work, *Karen* (1947), is a classic story of the pioneer heroine.

The story opens in Rendalen, Norway, where Karen spends her first years, happily cleaning, cooking and helping her Grandmother Storgaard. But after her grandmother's death and her parents' inefficient management of the farm, Karen and her sister Swanhild decide to go to America where an older brother has already emigrated. They settle first in Dubuque, Iowa, where Karen meets another Norwegian, Arne, whom she marries, and eventually she and her young husband homestead in Dakota Territory, enticed there by a fraudulent land company.

Karen is an enterprising young woman who loves her artistic, violin-playing husband very much, but does not consider him resourceful and strong-willed enough to survive alone on the Dakota prairie. She, however, has the qualities to be a successful pioneer — boundless energy for work, initiative, determination. When she and her sister arrive penniless and unable to speak English in Dubuque, she finds them jobs as cooks and maids in a Yankee family by simply knocking on doors. When she and Arne arrive at their claim and find they have been lied to by the land agent, Arne wants to return to Dubuque where at least he can give violin lessons to help them survive. Karen will have none of it. She looks at the barren land and the flimsy claim shack that was supposed to be their home and says, "We're not going back. We're going to stay right here. That land is good — it's wonderful in comparison with what even Grandmother Storgaard had in Norway. We can always get a house and other buildings. That only takes time and hard work" (132).

And work she does! She is determined to make it. In exchange for supplies, she bakes bread for the male settlers in town whose wives have not yet come to the prairie. She stands up to the cheating land agent — driving him off the claim with an axe when he comes to collect the horse and wagon he loaned them. She learns how to shoot a gun and kills a wolf while Arne is away procuring wood from the Big Sioux River. To keep herself busy while he is gone, she measures and cuts the wood for their barn. She encourages Arne to play his violin for the town dances in order to keep him satisfied living on the claim. She organizes a group of other Norwegian women to begin planning a church. She nurses Arne back to health after he develops a sore throat and high fever from being out in the blizzard. Pregnant with her first child, burdened with a sick husband, she struggles with chores and housework through their second hard winter. She even studies English when she has a spare moment. By the end of the story, when her son is born, Karen is confident and mature — a successful pioneer, a virtual superwoman. She loves the smell of the "upturned earth and dried weeds" that "seem to belong to the wild prairie" (154-55). She is a true pioneer heroine.

Almost all of the central characters in Borghild Dahl's later stories copy Karen in characteristics — although they do not use the prairie setting. In *Homecoming,* for instance, her heroine, Lyng, a Norwegian American who has grown up in much poverty in Minneapolis, takes her first teaching job in a small Norwegian community in northwest Minnesota. Dahl is particularly effective in describing authentic details of Norwegian-American life. Her cataloguing of Norwegian delicacies at festivals and parties is mouthwatering, and her analysis of the conflict between first and second generation Norwegians is insightful. Particularly revealing and sometimes harshly critical are the scenes in *Homecoming* of the narrow-minded Norwegian community in which Lyng teaches.

Dahl may have created her self-reliant and independent heroines out of values she herself learned as a child since most of her later books closely parallel incidents in her own life. She learned much from her father, who loved the United States intensely for the opportunity that it offered to become all one could become. He instilled that value in his daughter: " . . . to this day," she writes, "when I seem to be surrounded by insurmountable difficulties, I always remember that I can drill through mountains" ("My Norwegian Father"). For all of his enthusiasm for his new country, her father taught his children to be proud of their Norwegian heritage, too. He insisted that they learn to speak and read Norwegian and study Norwegian literature and music. "When I was granted a fellowship to study in Norway by the American Scandinavian Foundation," she wrote, "and when, years later, I was decorated by King Haakon with the St. Olaf medal, I was sorry that my father was not alive to share these honors with me. For I felt they were his almost more than mine" ("My Norwegian Father").

Two other books follow the narrative plan of *Karen* in recounting the pilgrimage from the homeland in Denmark or Norway to settlement on the South Dakota prairie. Inga Hansen Dickerson's *Trina* (1956) and Doris Stensland's *Haul the Water Haul the Wood* (1977) are both fictional works based on fact. Neither woman is a professional writer; consequently, the stories show weaknesses in character development and narrative structure. What the writers lack in literary skill they make up for in devotion to their subjects. Their stories are tributes to their love for these foremothers. Inga Hansen Dickerson cautions that the story of her mother Trina Bursen, who homesteaded near Yankton, is "too rose-colored," but, she says, she has never seen "the spots" on her mother's character any more than she has ever seen the spots on the sun (Foreword). Doris Stensland was inspired to write of her great grandmother Johanna Overseth, who homesteaded in Lincoln County, by a Biblical reference in her ancestor's hymnbook: "For our citizenship is in heaven" (Preface).

Like Karen, both Trina and Johanna thrive on hard work and the demands of life on the prairie in the seventies, eighties, and nineties. They display courage in facing the challenges of grasshoppers, illness, wild animals, loneliness, hungry Indians, drought and blizzards, and they are both determined that no hardships will drive them off their land. They are towers of strength to their families. They take pride in the homes they create, the churches they build, the butter they churn, the food and clothing they produce. They show leadership in organizing women's groups to support the church and to provide help to distressed neighbors. Particularly strong is their unshakable faith in God—and hard work. Benjamin Franklin was not more dedicated to the belief that success would follow in the way of individual industry, thrift, and efficient use of time than these sturdy pioneering women who gave themselves to establishing communities on the empty land. Their legacy is evident today in the energy of many women who give countless hours of work in support of community projects—cultural, educational, charitable.

While the Scandinavian women writers celebrated the opportunity, independence, and accomplishment that awaited them on the land, settlers with a Yankee background sometimes found ethnic diversity threatening to their customs and beliefs. Such conflict is examined in Willa Cather's work, but the South Dakota novel that most clearly exemplifies it is *The Land They Possessed* (1956), by Mary Worthy Breneman. This pseudonym represents the combined efforts of Mary Worthy Thurston, who was a teacher in Eureka, and her daughter Muriel Breneman, now living in Washington, D.C. (Schick). The women drew on their own family's history. The grandfather Joseph Worthy, the model for John Ward in the novel, ran a store in Ipswich and lived on a farm seventeen miles from town.

The story deals with the conflict between the Yankee settlers (the Wards), who come from the settled regions of the East to make it rich in the Dakota boom, and the German-Russian family (the Grosses), who sought to own land and hold it tenaciously.

Handsome, restless John Ward exhibits the spirit of the western adventurer, forever speculating on the growth and development of new towns, rather than the endurance of the homesteader, whose goal is to acquire land that would achieve the dream of a productive farm. John Ward hires help, runs a business in town, loves horses, and, finally, in anger at his daughter's marriage to a "foreigner"—a German-Russian—moves on to Montana over his wife's protests at building yet another new home in yet another new land.

In many ways, the Ward family values are typical of the first and second generation of writers who cherished their eastern gentility and culture. Like so many of the older wives and mothers in the earlier books by South Dakota women writers, Mavis Ward dislikes living on a homestead—commenting that she has not been off the place in over two years (Breneman 95). Furthermore, like Beret in *Giants in the Earth,* she fears the prairie—as her daughter Michal learns as they gaze over the empty prairie of their new claim. " 'I don't mind the winds so much,' " she tells another homesteader's wife who finally succumbs to the loneliness and loses her sanity, " 'but I miss the trees. The land seems so big—so bare and empty. John tells me I should see it as it will be . . . but I long for short distances and sheltering groves' " (23). Yet with Hetty to do the cooking and heavy work, Mavis maintains her prairie home as an oasis of eastern gentility in the empty wilderness—complete with Spode china, books, kid gloves, and a *pot pourri.* She is delighted when the family moves to Eureka to live in town: " ' . . . it'll be lovely to live in a peaceful little village where I can hear church bells ringing and stand in the door and watch the girls going to Sabbath school in their best clothes' " (108).

Mavis feels distinctly superior to the "Rooshans"—discouraging her daughter Michal's friendship with Katie Keim. She does not desire them as friends even when her brother Fred remonstrates with her: " ' . . . can't you see, Mavis . . . their type are the strong ones—the ones who'll possess the land. In a generation they'll be well off, and their children good Americans' " (31). But neither Mavis nor John Ward can accept this, and they caution Michal not to forget that " 'They [the German-Russians] aren't of our class' " (31). In fact, the "Rooshans" are regarded with disdain by most of the Anglo community—for their sheepskin coats and Astrakhan hats, the smells of their cooking, their feather beds and pillows, and their hard work in the fields.

Michal herself, the central figure of the novel, expresses some of the same snobbery as her mother early in the story. She is surprised when the Keim outhouse is as clean as her family's. She is outraged when John Ward drowns the mongrel puppies whelped by his purebred pointer, but she eventually feels the pedigreed Irish setter he buys her to replace the puppies is superior to the mongrel she had first loved. Yet Michal's prejudice is not firmly fixed and her love for her friend Katie ultimately demolishes it. When another "Englisher" calls Katie "a dirty Rooshan," she stoutly defends her: " 'Katie's not dirty! She's cleaner than you are!' " (125).

Because of its fully developed minor characters, *The Land They Possessed* has a richness of texture that most earlier works by South Dakota women authors do not have. Nonetheless, the story is Michal's and she is a genuine pioneer heroine. She is nine years old when the story opens and she grows up on the prairie, finally defying her family and running off to marry Karl Gross, the German-Russian boy who has attracted her since the day she first saw him walking with a group of German-Russians from the train that had brought them to Dakota Territory.

Like many earlier pioneer heroines, Michal loves the prairie—even though she understands her mother's fear of its bigness, emptiness, and loneliness. For Michal, it is alive with beauty—the cattails in the slough, the sound of the plover, trumpeter swan, wild geese, sandhill crane, and killdeer, and the splash of color from buttercups, pasque flowers, violets, prairie roses, clover, cone flowers, and goldenrod. She resorts to a pigweed patch near the claim for privacy and reflection, and she plants and nurtures willows by the dam with tender pride. When the family moves to Eureka, she finds "the place of the rock"—a buffalo wallow on top of a hill with a huge rock in the middle. To this place she flees when she is troubled and uncertain, when she is searching for herself, her being.

The Land They Possessed does not traffic in the usual school and outdoor adventures of most pioneer stories. Michal does not "do" in quite the same way as Karen or Trina or the heroines of earlier writers. Yet she grows and questions — challenging her parents' values in her friendship with Katie and in her defense of a dirty, ill-kempt child of a poor woman. She challenges the minister of the church in questions about God after the death of her beloved Uncle Fred. She longs to wear pants when she rides, concluding that " 'men have the best of it' " (190). She courageously fights a prairie fire even though her mother cautions her against it.

Yet it is in the strong sexual attraction Michal feels for Karl Gross that this story departs most radically from earlier versions of the genre. The book is obviously more frank in its exploration of Michal's fantasies about Karl who stirs her blood and captures her imagination and of her wonder at the physical changes in her body as she matures. She is troubled by the complexities of adult life, for her relationship with Karl is stormy. She finds Karl physically compelling — proud, arrogant, demanding, independent — yet she wants to be dominated by him no more than she wants to be dominated by her father. She becomes engaged to Lewis Reid, the banker's son, but she cannot resist Karl's passion, and the two elope, entering a marriage that promises to be tempestuous but enduring, because of the strengths of the two characters.

Michal is a pioneer heroine because she chooses finally to embrace the "foreign" culture and to bloom on the prairie where she has been planted. She has the qualities that will enable her to survive, to triumph as Karl's wife on a farm of their own. She does not, like her mother and father, escape to Montana, but puts down her roots and thrives, because of her love of the land, her independence, and her courage.

Another third generation writer set her pioneer story in more modern times. Anne Holland, the narrator and central character in Verna Moxley's *Wind 'til Sundown* (1954) moves with her husband and children from Michigan to an abandoned homestead on Sioux Indian land. Automobiles, electricity, and telephones exist to ease the burdens of some farms, but they are of little use in the trackless west river country where Anne and her family settle. The run-down farmhouse has no adequate water, and the young couple has only their hope, their energy, their strength, and their courage in the first six months as they struggle to build a ranch.

Although Anne loves the spring mornings and the summer sunsets, she fights the same battles as earlier pioneer women — loneliness, brutally hard work, drought, hail, scorching heat, sudden winter blizzards, and, always, the wind. The harsh conditions of ranch life appall her and she is terrified of isolation on the empty land. "Fear — fear — fear, always stalking my footsteps. . . . " she writes (Moxley 200). She resists the demands pioneer life makes on her — at one point deciding to ask John to give up and go to California. But she does not. Instead, through the example of the other ranch women she meets, and through her own determination and will, she conquers her fears and triumphs. She rides alone across the prairie at night to get help for the ailing cattle; she drives an old car through gumbo to town in order to save her baby; she succeeds in persuading the well diggers to come. Finally, she emerges as a mature woman with a clear sense of herself, exhibiting the same independence, physical courage, and initiative that earlier pioneer heroines demonstrated. Even in more modern settings, the *idea* of pioneer life as a setting for the maturation of a young woman into a full-fledged heroine has potency for a woman writer.

Among other books by women writers after World War II that are set in South Dakota, one particularly demands discussion — Marian Castle's *Deborah* (1946).[5] Although the writer is an Iowan, she taught school in South Dakota for some years and set the beginning and ending of her novel on a South Dakota homestead near the imaginary town of Black Willow. More important, the novel spans three generations, opening when Deborah Seerlie is a seventeen-year-old living with her parents on the south central Dakota prairie in the 1890s and ends when she returns to the farm in the 1930s with her granddaughter Linda to reclaim the family land in the Dust Bowl years. Without expressing it precisely in words, Marian Castle dramatically and persuasively illustrates the power of pioneer experience in contributing to the development of an independent, self-possessed young woman. Though not a pioneer herself, this writer was attracted to the *idea* of a pioneer heroine. She artistically created a character shaped by the prairie environment who returns to the source of her strength on South Dakota soil in order to nurture yet another generation of heroines in her granddaughter.

When the story opens, Deborah Seerlie is a bright, pretty, ambitious young woman, little influenced by her pioneering parents who hope she will marry a local farm boy and settle in the neighborhood. Deborah has other goals, especially after her pride is hurt when a visiting educated easterner laughs at her because she does not know the difference between the James brothers who robbed trains in the West and the James brothers (Henry and William) who wrote learned books and novels in the East. She is determined to acquire education and culture and is all eagerness when she stands on her favorite rise on the prairie flatland watching a tumbleweed roll whispering, " 'Oh, wait for me. . . . Can't you see, I'm coming too. . . . ' " (Castle 42). Deborah resembles the first generation of pioneer heroines in the attraction that education and culture hold for her, but she also, like them, finds solace in the endless sweep of land and sky.

Deborah loses her way, however, in her pursuit of these goals. After going to Gideon College for a year, she leaves because of her mother's illness and family's financial limitations and teaches school in another small Dakota town. She marries the school superintendent, a good-looking, rather weak and self-centered man, who does not succeed professionally, moving from school to school, finally dying of pneumonia when he is on the verge of being fired from the school in the small Iowa town of Waukauna. Forced on her own resources as a widow with three young children, Deborah marries again—this time for financial security. Ira Laing does not have "A Degree" but is a successful contractor and a good stepfather, providing Deborah with the money to acquire the "culture" and "education" she has sought. Unfortunately, she mistakes superficial appearances for genuine learning—putting a high value on "proper English," membership in the Fortnightly Literary Club, and "social advantages for her children." She confuses social position and wealth with erudition and knowledge of the world.

All of Deborah's dreams come to nothing. Her son dies in the flu epidemic after running away to join the army in World War I. Her two daughters do not finish the expensive colleges she sends them to but choose to live in Chicago according to the dictates of the "new freedom" for women of the 1920s. They are "Bohemians" — smoking, drinking bootleg liquor, living in an apartment and working in advertising, idolizing Edna St. Vincent Millay, flirting with ideas of Freud and Marx, and falling in love with men who do not intend to marry them. The independence that Gay and Arden seek is not, Deborah becomes painfully aware, the freedom that her generation of young women longed for. Even their liberated whirl ends disastrously for Deborah when her daughter Gay dies giving birth to an illegitimate daughter. The baby is cared for by Arden, the sister, until she is unable to continue because of her husband's ill health. When Deborah's husband, Ira, also dies, she is alone and aging, aware that her struggle for "education" and "culture" has brought her more pain than joy. The depression has made her poor, and she has to look after her twelve-year-old granddaughter, Linda, since the child's father has to go to the Southwest to arrest his tuberculosis.

Together, Deborah and Linda return to the South Dakota farm, but it is even bleaker than in Deborah's childhood. The depression and dust grip South Dakota: "Everywhere the dust lay in dunes. Fences were covered over with drifts of fine powdery dirt like brown snow" (312). Linda is afraid of the sound of howling coyotes at first, and Deborah is overwhelmed at the task of cleaning the old, neglected farm house and repairing the barn. Nonetheless, she bolsters Linda's courage and tackles the chores cheerfully, and the two find a dogged satisfaction in "making do." Deborah is back in the privation and challenge of pioneer life that demands hard work, ingenuity, and resourcefulness of women and gives them a sense of their own worth. A dust blizzard ultimately tests both women. Deborah has to find a way to the barn to pull a calf from their suffering but precious cow, and she falls and loses her way on the return.

Linda, using a clothesline tied to the house to keep her direction in the blinding storm, finds her grandmother and leads her home:

> She must get together at least half as much spunk as the young-one had, Deborah scolded herself, and smiled up at her granddaughter. She saw the shine of anxious sweat on the child's dust-streaked forehead. She's scared stiff, but she wasn't going to let on, thought Deborah admiringly.
> "You saved my life," she said simply.
> Linda looked proud and relieved . . . . (341)

Another young woman, three generations after settlement, becomes a heroine on the prairie.

The two women live together successfully on the farm until Linda is ready for college. This time, both Linda and the young man she intends to marry at the end of World War II will go off together. But most important, Deborah sees and understands the strong, resourceful young woman Linda has become as a "child of pioneers." In the final scenes the young woman changes a tire, drives into town, manages the farm, and looks after her grandmother with equal assurance. When Deborah says she wishes she could have provided more "advantages," Linda responds:

> "Why, Granny, you gave me *every* advantage. Outdoor advantages — like pig-raising and carpentering . . . . Indoor advantages like — oh, like making poems and watercolor sketches and piecrust. You scrimped to get me through high school, and you kept after me to study for exams — what more could any girl ask?" (368)

In Linda's words, Marian Castle has neatly summarized the feelings of many women on the Dakota frontier. All three generations of writers created, in fact or in imagination, the *idea* of the pioneer heroine. So powerful was the concept that it flourished abundantly in the writings of South Dakota women for over half a century. The first generation of writers recounted their own stories. The second generation returned in memory to experience again the time when they discovered their true selves. And, finally, the third generation recreated the story, like myth, out of their imagination when it is no longer the fact of the pioneer heroine that has meaning but the idea itself. Why so long after the historical event does this story still have immediacy and meaning for women? One can speculate that the pioneer experience appeals to women as a chance to grow, to develop, to learn, to be without artificial restrictions or conventions imposed by a society encrusted with tradition. If the American male finds the cowboy image appealing because he is not "fenced in," the American female may find the pioneer heroine appealing because she is not "fenced in" by notions of what a woman could not or should not do. Long after settlement had re-established conventions and traditions that restricted a woman's choices and opportunities, the idea of pioneer experience nourished her soul, her sense of herself. We can be grateful that these books enable us also to be nourished from the same source.

NOTES

[1]See Barbara Welter, "The Cult of True Womanhood: 1820-1860," *American Quarterly* 18 (1966): 151-62, 173-74.

[2]See Zitkala-Ša, "Impressions of an Indian Childhood," *Atlantic Monthly* Jan. 1900: 37-44. "The School Days of an Indian Girl," *Atlantic Monthly* Feb. 1900; "An Indian Teacher Among Indians," *Atlantic Monthly* March 1900; "The Soft-Hearted Sioux," *Harper's Monthly Magazine* March 1901: 505-08; *Old Indian Legends* (Boston: Ginn, 1901); *American Indian Stories* (Washington: Hayworth, 1921).

[3]For a fuller treatment of the first generation of writers, see Ruth Ann Alexander, "South Dakota Women Writers and the Emergence of the Pioneer Heroine," *South Dakota History* 13 (1983): 177-205.

[4]For a fuller treatment of the second generation of writers, see Ruth Ann Alexander, "South Dakota Women Writers and the Blooming of the Pioneer Heroine 1922-1939," *South Dakota History* 14 (1984): 281-307.

[5]Other works are Verna and Bill Cleaves, *Dust of the Earth* (Philadelphia and New York: Lippincott, 1975); Olive Elsie Knox, *Mrs. Minister* (Philadelphia: Westminster, 1956); Winnie Crandall Saunders, *Daughters of Dakota* (Caldwell, Idaho: Caxton, 1960); Libbie Williams, *Memories of the Black Hills: A Story of Betty West* (New York: Vantage, 1956).

WORKS CITED

Breneman, Mary Worthy. *The Land They Possessed.* 1956. Bismarck, N.D.: Germans from Russia Heritage Society, 1984.

Castle, Marian. *Deborah.* New York: William Morrow, 1946.

Dahl, Borghild. *Karen.* New York: Random, 1947.

– – –. "My Norwegian Father Taught Me to Love the United States." *Minneapolis Tribune* 26 Jan. 1980, morning ed.: 5B.

Dickerson, Inga Hansen. *Trina.* New York: Comet, 1956.

Garland, Hamlin. *Main-Travelled Roads.* New York: Signet, 1962.

Moxley, Verna. *Wind 'til Sundown.* Caldwell, Idaho: Caxton, 1954.

Schick, Lenora. Letter to Ruth Ann Alexander. 5 July 1985.

Stensland, Doris. *Haul the Water Haul the Wood.* Aberdeen, S.D.: North Plains, 1977.

The Mystique of Siouxland

FREDERICK MANFRED

Frederick Manfred lives in Luverne, Minnesota, where he writes novels, short stories, and poetry. This reminiscence was given at the 1985 Humanities Seminar at Augustana College.

When I'm on a trip for any length of time, it isn't long before I become homesick for Siouxland. I didn't do what Lewis and Fitzgerald and Hemingway did — run off to Paris to find a place where they could feel at home. I never felt at home on either coast. When I was getting ready to give this talk, I was wondering why that was, and so for a week or so, off and on, and especially in the forenoon, I sat alone in my study, my tipi as I call it, and tried to figure it out. I made a review of my whole life, like you do just before you're about to die.

To start from the beginning, in my sophomore year at Western Academy in Hull, Iowa, a denominational school, my father told me he didn't have the money to send me to high school. He could pay for the tuition, but I had to scramble for the rest. I decided to go anyway. I did manage to borrow some money for my textbooks from my uncles, who weren't sure that I should go to high school, but who liked me. I learned that a neighbor boy rode to the Hull High School in a horse and buggy and I could ride with him for a dollar a week. But after about three weeks, I noticed that he had me driving the horse while he'd run behind the buggy because he was on the track team. He was going to be a long-distance cross-country runner. Well, I liked to run myself. So we'd tie up the reins and we'd both run behind the buggy. But here I was paying one dollar a week to run. That wasn't exactly good business. So after a while I quit my arrangement with him and ran by myself.

It was seven and a half miles to the high school and seven and a half miles back. Except for January and February, when it was too cold, I ran that all year long. The last half-mile home, there were three little hills. About a minute or two before I'd show up over those hills, my best friend, Rover, our dog, would go sit on the porch and look for me. When my head would bob over the first hill, my dog would sit up alert; the second hill, more alert; the third hill, he'd give a little yip, jump off the porch and run up the road and meet me, and, in ecstasy, would circle me. He wasn't supposed to jump on me because he might be muddy and I'd get my schoolgoing clothes dirty, so he learned how to come close and lick my fingertips, and then make another circle around me. Well, that kind of welcome, you know, you never forget. It burns deep into you when even the dog likes your coming home.

My brothers, of course, were the same way. They wanted to know what I'd learned in high school. They were younger, and high school was a mysterious world to them. I'd come home with strange books: a Latin book that they couldn't understand, and a grammar book, which, of course, was a real mystery to them.

I went on to Calvin College when I was eighteen. My mother wouldn't let me go when I was sixteen because she felt I wasn't ready for the fleshpots of Grand Rapids, Michigan. So I stayed home two years. By the time I went to Calvin, I'd pretty well forgotten any grammar that I had in high school. The English teacher in high school hadn't really liked me. The only reason he said he passed me was because I was his best Shakespeare student, but when it came to grammar I was pretty bad. I didn't realize what was going on, that I was using the American language and not formal English.

When I ran into Miss Timmer, my freshman English teacher at Calvin, I hit my bugaboo. She had the curious habit of keeping all the papers till the end of the semester, so you didn't know how you were doing. When I returned after Christmas vacation (I had caught a ride home for those two weeks to be with my brothers and my father; my mother had by this time died), I found this whole packet of papers in my room which a friend of mine had left there. It was from Miss Timmer. I started going through it. (I probably should tell you what Miss Timmer looked like. She wore low heels and military dress, and she had a slight moustache.) I started going through those papers and saw all kinds of red marks on them. I didn't get too disturbed over that; I knew what I wrote wasn't very good for the kind of English she wanted from me. But when I got to the term paper, I saw that she'd read only halfway and then had stopped and written, "Dear Mr. Feikema, there's no reason for me to read any further. There are too many mistakes to pass you." Then she signed her name.

Instantly, a wave of homesickness came over me. I remembered the dog licking my fingers. I remembered my brothers. What was I doing there? I decided to give up the idea that I would ever be a writer.

I had everything pretty well packed and was going to hitchhike home in a snowstorm, when a fellow from Sioux Center, Iowa, Edward Bierma, a junior, happened to come into my room to tell stories. He asked, "Where are you going?" I said, "I'm going home." And when I explained to him why and showed him those papers, he took me by the arm and walked me over to Wealthy Street and bought me some glazed doughnuts, which he knew I loved, and some coffee. By the time he got me back to the dorm, he had talked me into staying. He said, "We'll help you." Of course, that meant someone would help me write my papers. I knew that he couldn't very well help me. He was going into law, and law students have a peculiar way of thinking and writing that is alien to me.

What I finally did to lick the problem was to ape Miss Timmer's manners. I had class with her at eight o'clock and had a free hour afterwards. The moment I was through with class, I went to my room and, with her image in my mind to the point where I would get up from my chair and walk around like she did, on the back of her low heels, I'd write my essay for the next day. I gave back exactly the manner she gave me. I didn't pay any attention to the content of what she said. I just remembered how she said things.

There was a lot of consternation on the campus, by the way, that she was going to flunk me. The basketball coach had spotted me walking across campus one day, and he decided that he had to have me on his team. I said, "Well, I can't play basketball. I've never played it." He said, "I saw you play baseball the other day and you know round objects. You're six-foot-eight, and you won't even have to jump; you can pick all the rebounds off. And you won't have to jump to get the tip." (In those days, after every basket you had to run back to center for a tipoff.) He went to the president—the president had taken a liking to me—and between the two of them, they talked Miss Timmer into giving me a conditional instead of a flunk, only if I improved the second semester.

Well, when I started to ape her manner, her talk, her enunciation, and so on, I suddenly started getting ecstatic little notes at the end of each paper I handed in. "Dear Mr. Feikema, You're improving. Splendid!" And I wound up, I think, with an *A* because she averaged the whole thing out, the flunk with the *A*, and I got a *C+* for both semesters. So the record doesn't show I flunked; it just says I got a *C+* in English first semester.

The next thing that happened in my life to make me terribly homesick was when I hitchhiked to New York with no money in my pocket. I finally wound up in New Jersey at the U.S. Rubber Company. I got the job with them because they needed a big center for their team. Every day I had to work inside where the air was full of flying soapstone. I began to cough. Knowing that soapstone wasn't good for me—that eventually it would kill me—I began to think about going home. I worked there from March until August 1935, and then one day went in and quit my job. I then learned from the management that the personnel department had spotted me and had decided that they were going to work me up the ladder. But I left anyway.

I first went to Boston, where I was promptly pickpocketed. All the money I'd so far saved up! Once again I thought of home. They didn't do those things in Doon, Iowa. I went to

Washington, D.C., where I stopped going west at my aunt's house. Her husband worked in the navy yards, was a World War I vet, and every now and then showed it. He had been in a gas attack and had survived. My aunt thought I should apply for jobs with my representative and senator from Iowa. But I got the run-around from those people. It was my first experience about how nice they can talk to you when you're visiting with them, but how little they do for you after you leave their office. From there I finally went straight home.

One of the things I noticed, by the way, when hitchhiking, was that I always got a ride. I always made it a point to be well dressed, wearing a Calvin red sweater with a big *C* gold letter. Most of the salesmen who stopped to give me a ride looked at me to see if I'd fit in their small car. And if I could, then I was to drive.

Once I was picked up by a very beautiful girl in Iowa City who took me to Council Bluffs. It took her all day because she had to make stops in various towns. She was a saleslady for lingerie. I had an invitation from her to stay over the weekend and look for a job at the *Omaha Bee*. I was shocked and rejected the offer.

By this time, my father had moved to Perkin's Corner, Iowa. And once again I had a great time with my brothers. One of the reasons I loved my brothers so much was that they were always playing games. In the summertime we played baseball endlessly, using the chicken coop as a backstop. In the wintertime we had cob fights, which were always great sport. We had the cob fights in the haymow. In fact we tried to do the chores early so that between five and six, when Dad went in to get a cup of coffee, we had an hour to play. Cob fights were deliciously exciting because we learned after a while that if we went down into the horse barn and took the cobs out of the mangers, where the horses had just finished nibbling the kernels off them, the cobs would still be wet with real wonderful slobber. And if you broke the wet cobs in half they made great weapons. When they landed, you felt it. We'd crawl through the hay up over the top to the hay carrier. We'd crawl everywhere. I had told them about James Fenimore Cooper, and so we played out the great stories of Chingachgook and Deerslayer.

My youngest brother, Henry, was two years old when his mother died. Those years, when I stayed home from school, I used to carry him on my shoulders. When I'd be cultivating, I'd take him to the field and have him sit with his legs around my neck. Or when I walked over the yard feeding the hogs or the cows, he'd sit up there. I was the one who housebroke him. I'd point out to him how wet my collar got. He learned that wasn't a good thing to do. Through all those various adventures you can see why there was much here in Siouxland.

There are other reasons, too, why home was so magical. I had heroes at home. My father was one. One time I came home from high school — the year when I was running every day — and came flying into the kitchen to find my dad sitting by the stove, his feet up on the reservoir, where we kept the water warm, his hand over his nose and his usual pipe and cup of coffee standing nearby. My mother looked up from her ironing, and said, "Yes, son, your father's taken to jumping off windmills." Mother never was sarcastic. That was alien to her. So I knew something bad had happened. And all Dad said was, "You're gonna have to do the chores alone tonight. The team of horses is still tied to the fence by the windmill."

After I'd changed clothes, I went out to see what had happened. I looked up the ladder of our wooden windmill and saw that the three top rungs had broken out. I looked down at the ground and saw where his heels had hit and where his nose had landed a little further down the line. The windmill was thirty-eight feet high. He survived the fall because he was a very fast thinker. My mother's brothers thought he was a dumbbell, but we'd always known he was extremely keen and extremely fast. He could read your mind before you got into trouble. We have now figured out he had dyslexia. In an emergency, where he didn't have to go through academic channels, the learned word, he went directly to the point. He did it instinctively and quickly.

He told me later how it happened. "When the first rung broke," he said, "I grabbed the second one with both hands. When that broke, I grabbed the third one. But when that broke, I knew that if I hit one of those cross beams below I was done. So I kicked myself out as far as I could. Then, as I was going down, I thought, well, how am I going to land? I remembered how grasshoppers landed. So I bent my legs like a grasshopper, hit the ground, and bounced forward." Now that's fast thinking!

There was another occasion, before I was born, when my dad was quick, or I wouldn't be here. He was shingling the roof of a round barn. (The barn is still there, northeast of Doon, Iowa.) He was shingling the cupola, when the board he was standing on gave way and he started to slide down. "I was slidding off the roof," he said, "when I remembered there was a fresh cowpile slightly to the left of where I was sliding. I rolled over and managed to get far enough over to land right in it, forty feet below, and survived." That took quick thinking, too, and a good memory of where the cowpile was.

On another occasion, I helped my father with the cornpicking machine, the year of the great wind, when a lot of the ears had fallen to the earth—about a third of them. So my brother Edward and I ran after the cornpicker and snapped up the loose ears and threw them in the curve where the chain comes by, and they would go into the machine and get cleaned. About ten o'clock we stopped for some coffee in a jug. All too soon it was time to roll again. Dad got up on his throne. He had five horses on the picker, and each horse had its own line. He said "giddap" a couple of times, but the horses didn't move. They had chilled off. Finally, he said, "Ed, go pick up a clod and hit Nell." (Nell was the lead horse.) Ed picked up a clod and threw it. At the same time that the clod hit, my father said, "Giddap!" Nell started to pull. The machine swung over to the left and picked up Ed's leg where he was standing. Father saw it instantly and let go with one of the most chilling "whoa's" I've ever heard in my life. The horses stopped, stiff. And there was Ed, caught in the gathering lugs. Dad sat very still, very quietly. He said, "Fred, take off Queen." She was the wildest horse we had. So I unhitched her and tied her to the fence behind us. I took off Daise. I took off Dick. I took off Maude. Finally, I took off Nell. When I had all the horses tied to the fence, my father broke down crying.

When his eyes cleared, we got the wrenches out and spent the rest of the forenoon taking the machine apart and getting Ed's leg out. He was safe. There were just a couple of little gouges into the muscle part. Again, the swiftness of that man was remarkable. A hero!

I also had hero uncles: my mother's two brothers. Uncle Henry was a marvelous ball player. He was three years older than me, sort of my older brother, very independent, casual. When he walked on to the diamond, his air was always, well, it was okay if the other team played nine innings for a little batting practice, but Doon had already won. A couple of times when I got the bases loaded, he'd walk over from his shortstop position and say, "You know, we're not going to get this game done before dark the way you're loading the bases." Or he'd say, "You know this looks like you don't care. What's going on here?" He always had a little quip.

Uncle Hank was also that way. Uncle Herm lived with Uncle Hank for a number of years. Visiting them you never knew quite where you stood, if they were teasing you or if they were telling you the truth. It was tough to decide what was going on with those two fellows. I loved the way they did life.

I was the oldest child, and my mother felt, since my father couldn't read, the oldest child should read the Bible at table worship. I read the Bible in Dutch three times through from the age of seven on, and then later on I read it through three more times in English, King James Version. Also, I often asked if I could have the Bible and go read a little by myself. I'd read Job, Ruth—all those wonderful tales in the Old Testament.

When we'd go visiting—and in those days whole families went visiting whole families—I always had two questions: "Do they have a little boy there that I can chum around with? And do you think they have some books in their parlor?" If there were books in the parlor, I didn't care about the chum. I would take the book and read awhile there, and then take it home with me. Gradually, I started to learn that there were books about the area.

When I was out of college and sitting home on my father's porch just east of Doon one summer, Dad took a long siesta and I got out Rölvaag's *Giants in the Earth*. As I read along, it suddenly dawned on me the Per Hansa's trek could have come over the very farm I was sitting on. My country was celebrated! It was sacred! Just as sacred as the English land was for the English people with their *Beowulfs,* Spensers, Shakespeares, Doughtys, and Conrads. An explosion in my head! Some more proof that this was wonderful country to be from.

Later on I discovered that Ruth Suckow had lived in Hawarden, Iowa, where her father was a minister. She'd written a great novel about Iowa called *The Folks.* And then I found out that Herbert Quick lived southeast of Sioux City; he wrote a book called *Vandemark's Folly,* a fine Dutch title. I learned that in Sioux City a man named Hiram Chittenden, an army officer, wrote what is still today the true picture of the history of the fur trade in the old far west. And there was Harvey Dunn, who did the painting called *Woman at the Pump.* So we had some topnotch artists celebrating the area I had come from. That made it even more precious.

Then came the day when I really started to write. I had the problem of trying to write in such a way that someone from some distance away wouldn't get the idea that this was a vast country I was writing about. If I'd say Sioux City, it would be in Iowa. If I'd say Worthington, it would be in Minnesota. If I'd say Sioux Falls, it would be in South Dakota. Or if I mentioned Norfolk, it would be in Nebraska. Four big states! Actually, you know, those cities are only an hour and a half apart. This is a very cohesive area. So I decided that I should name the area. I also remembered very distinctly that no one had ever mentioned they were going to Sioux Falls, South Dakota. They just said Sioux Falls. Or they said I'm going to Sioux City, or I'm going to Norfolk, or I'm going to Worthington. There was no mention of states. If you watched the marriage statistics, you noticed after a while that Dutchmen were marrying Norwegians, Norwegians were marrying Germans, and so on. A slow but sure mix was going on. Also, most people here were Protestants.

I cast around for all kinds of names. I had two pages of names written down. By the way, I've discovered that if you're going to title something, you should not pick it the first time you see a likely candidate. You should put it down, and then someday casually pick up the list of candidates, and whatever catches your eye, that's probably the right one. I had "Lord Grizzly" written down a month before I finally chose it. But it didn't stick out until one day I happened to pick up the list and the phrase "Lord Grizzly" came right off the page at me. It takes awhile for the back of your head or the bottom of your head to decide what's right. You see, willy-nilly you often have to use the formal English you learned from teachers, and the formal English you learn from critics, and the confused English of lawyers and legislators. It takes awhile to keep that best part of you, the lizard part of you, alert for the right things.

The one name that finally stuck out was "Sioux-land." Well, I was never much in favor of hyphens, so after a while I eliminated the hyphen and called it Siouxland. This occurred in the late summer of 1945. I drew up a map and kept revising that map through 1946, while preparing the final draft of my book *This Is the Year*. Then, in April 1947, *This Is the Year* was printed, and the publishers used that map on the endpapers of the book.

Within a year I started hearing the Sioux City radios say, "Serving greater Siouxland." It saved them the same problem that I had of naming all four states each time, when everybody knew that we were all one people in this great valley of the Big Sioux. The newspapers began using it. We had such things as the Siouxland Conference. Sioux City used it the most often.

It is with some regret, though, that the advertisers in Sioux Falls started calling it the Sioux Empire instead of Siouxland. And that's really quite ridiculous. Indians didn't believe in empires. They are a little bit like my own people, the Frisians. It's hard to get the Frisians organized into bands. About the Frisians they say: "If you have one man and his family, you have a church. If you have two men and their families, you have a schism. And if you have three men and their families, you have three provinces." They can't agree. Indians are somewhat the same way. They're very suspicious of anyone that takes on leadership. In the Indian world you only have leaders for a given project. When it was time to get some buffalo, the council would pick a guy to head the hunt. And he'd be the head man for a while. But the moment the hunt was over, he went back to being just a brave.

The morals of the Sioux were similar to the morals of the Dutch Reformed. Take the seventh commandment. One Yankton Indian lady, who helped me with *Conquering Horse,* told me she didn't like the book. My face fell because I wanted her to like it. And when I finally pinned her down, she said, "Well, you whites think we Sioux women are loose. But the truth is we're stricter than you Dutch Reformed people." It was assumed that all girls would remain virgins until they were married. I said, "Well, apart from that, what did you think of the book?" She said, "Oh, it was fine."

All along I sensed that there were mysteries in the place. As a little boy I saw Sioux caravans going from Flandreau down Highway 75 (in those days it was called the King's Trail) through Pipestone to Sioux City, where they crossed the river and went to their friends' and their relatives' at Santee, Nebraska. And, contrariwise, I used to see the Santee Sioux come up with their caravans to Flandreau and to Pipestone. They went past our place. It was a familiar sight to see little Indian kids and the women folk stop along the road to pick herbs, tea, plums, and so on. My mother learned from an Indian woman that wild bergamot makes great tea.

In talking to the old people, both Indian and white, I learned that the burial mounds in northwest Iowa had to be a special place. They now think that there are some 250 mounds there, though there are some people who think that there are as many as 450. They are called the Blood Run Mounds. When my grandfather showed me the place, he pointed out a serpent mound — what was left of it. Dr. Dale Henning, of Luther College, in Decorah, has trouble believing there was a serpent mound. He can't find the evidence for it. Even if you fly over it it doesn't show up. I think what has happened is that the plow and the weather — frost and rain and wind — cut it down.

Something special had to have happened there in the past. They now think that some people were there as early as 6000 years ago. A railroad engineer, in his report, as well as on his map, indicated there was an amphitheater there—even playgrounds for games. This past summer, Dr. Henning found some 500 cache pits there, filled with debris. He opened about a tenth of them and found all kinds of marvelous things, which perhaps go back to the Omaha Indians around the year 800.

North of my place I kicked through some pocket gopher mounds on an island in Lake Benton, and I was struck by what I saw: broken buffalo bones, various points, and chips. I sent them to Eldon Johnson, the state archaeologist, in St. Paul. He promptly sent out a crew and, with careful carbon dating, they decided that some people had lived there 6000 years ago. Since that's north of Blood Run, and since there are mounds up and down all these rivers, there has to be some kind of connection. Then there is that turtle effigy, four miles north and a mile and a half east of Corson. It's almost gone now. But someone had carved or cut the outline of a turtle in a sort of plaza of Sioux quartzite. When was that cut there? Wonderful mystery. I've often sat above it trying to imagine who did it. And sometimes I see them—vague, fleeting—for a second.

Then up on top of the Blue Mounds, where I lived for fifteen years, I discovered a row of stones in deep grass. To my astonishment, when I picked up the top stones, the top of them was covered with lichen, but the bottom wasn't. When you'd look under those stones, none of the stones below them had lichen on them. That had to be old. One morning I wanted to see if the contractor had put my little writing shack true east and west. I knew I would have to check it on 21 September, give or take twelve hours. I looked past the cabin and saw that he was off a few inches. Out of curiosity, I walked over to the wire fence north of that and looked, and that was off quite a bit, about eleven feet to the length of that row of stones. Then I came back and stepped on the stones and looked east; there was the sun right on top of that row of stones. I thought, "Hey, no white man knew about that at the time." When the surveyors came through, they surveyed the country as if the earth was flat. And so they made errors. That's why we have all these jogs in the road between Rock Rapids and Luverne, and in the old days between Luverne and Brandon. But whoever put that row of stones there knew something about stars, true east and west. And where would they have found that information? Well, the people who built the mounds came from the Missouri River. They had to have been acquainted with the people in Cahokia, Illinois. Archaeologists have uncovered a Woodhenge down there that's a little larger than Stonehenge in England. It struck me one day that perhaps that row of stones behind my house was connected with those people. It was the only explanation I had. In any case, it makes for a marvelous mystery to unravel someday.

Another wonderful mystery to me was to discover that the geologists think that right where I had my home on Blue Mounds there once was a mountain range higher than Mount Everest. It ran from Mankato to Mitchell. Two glaciers worked at it and the second glacier finally managed to shove it off and push it all south. But it couldn't take the Blue Mounds down because that's solid Sioux quartzite five miles deep.

I remember hearing stories from my great uncles that when they first came here they ran into a lot of British. I began to look into that and ran across a fine book called *The British in Iowa,* written by Jacob Van der Zee. It turns out that in LeMars, Iowa, there was a whole British colony of second sons of very rich families in England. The older son and the father or the older sister didn't want those second sons around, so they sent them to America and supported them with a remittance.

I drove to LeMars one day and asked around. And, yes, there was the son of one left. His name was George Hotham. I looked him up. He had never married. His house was full of English things. His father had married a German maid. Before I went down I looked him up in *Burke's Peerage.* The entry read, "George P. Hotham, LeMars, Iowa, U.S.A., no issue." After visiting with him for a while, I said, "George, aren't you worried your particular branch of the Hotham family has no descendants?" Now here was a man who had cataracts, was in his seventies, had a Bertrand Russell nose, and spoke elegant English. He said, "I'm still looking." They told stories about him, how he liked to watch the girls walk by to high school in the morning. I asked him if he'd ever done any work. "No," he said, "never have." "Don't you clean up the house?" "No. In our family, we don't do work."

The British Hotham family went almost broke in World War II, and they couldn't send him any more remittance. But he didn't say anything. People didn't see him up town anymore. They made inquiry and discovered he had been literally starving to death. He'd been eating old crackers. So the businessmen of LeMars got together and put him on their payroll. The last years of his life he lived on social security, so he became an American remittance man. I thought that all rather wonderful.

What have we got today as compared to what we had when I was a boy? I grew up on a farm where the only engine was a four-horse pounder. No cars, no telephones, no radios, no phonograph. When Dad showed up with a chain-drive Overland one day, that was one of the great sights of my life. A little later on we got a phonograph, an Edison, with heavy, thick records. It was the first time I'd ever heard semi-classical music. Next came the telephone. There were eight patrons to a line, and each wall phone had batteries in it. I remember that when my father wanted to call somebody in town he had to call central. He'd ring and tell central who he wanted. Then he'd wait a minute and he'd say, "All right, you rubberneckers, there's seven of you on the line. Get off. I can't hear a thing." There'd be a little silence and then he'd say, "All right, Mrs. Murray, I know you're still on there. Get off."

When my mother died, in his grief, Dad bought a new Brunswick radio. Then, for the first time, not only could we hear *Amos 'n' Andy,* but we could hear WOI in Ames (that's Iowa spelled backwards without the *A*), or WOW in Omaha, or WCCO in Minneapolis. And if we were lucky, some nights we could get New York or Pittsburgh or Los Angeles. We heard symphony music, great long symphonies. That was my first exposure to symphonies. They reminded me of Dutch songs, which are sung very slowly. That was in 1929. Slowly, but surely, we entered into the modern world.

Today, in forty mintues, I can drive from my house in Luverne to Sioux Falls by taking the freeway. In the old days that would have taken all day in a horse and buggy. When we hauled livestock to the Sioux Falls stockyards, that was a whole day's drive. We loaded the hogs in the morning, drove in and took them to the commissioner's, had lunch in town and then went home. I never dreamed then that it would be possible to sit in a tractor and in two days do all the fall and spring plowing. In the old days with the Emerson doubleplow, it took me from about 10 August to the time to start high school to do the plowing.

Luverne now has a playhouse and a repertory theater, and they put on four good shows a year. I've noticed that other towns now have playhouses. And if we don't like the plays locally, we can ride to Minneapolis to the Guthrie Theater. If the music we hear isn't superb at the local symphony, we can drive to the Twin Cities and hear the Minnesota Orchestra.

The best part is the libraries. Doon had no library. I had to get books from my doctor. The doctor's wife took a liking to me and she let me read all of James Fenimore Cooper and Jack London those two years I stayed home between high school and college. Western Academy had just 1000 books in the whole library. I've noticed that the Luverne library now has a room twice this size full of books for students to read. They have 42,519 adult books available. Astonishing! Augustana has a fine library. And if you want a certain book they don't have, you can get it by interlibrary loan. Here in Siouxland! By mail I read forty magazines a year, all the way from literature to quantum mechanics to politics. When I get through with the magazines, by the way, I turn them over to the local library. I can sit here in Siouxland and have everything they have in New York or on the West Coast if I want it. When I was young, there were no well-read, brilliant friends to talk to. But now every town has one or two ornery cusses who read a little and dispute what the city hall does and ask embarrassing questions of the mayor. You can find the same kind of people here for intellectual fun, as I call it, as you can anywhere in New York.

I often stay at the Players, in New York, a club for writers and actors. Hemingway and Steinbeck, by the way, were members at one time. I discovered to my amazement I'm better read than many members are. Not just the magazines, but all kinds of books. So I can have everything that the East and West Coasts have, plus what I've got here: clear air and well-washed, sun-washed faces.

Last night, for example, we all had a marvelous time with Robert Bly. Over and over again I wished I had sat in an audience listening to Robert Bly in my youth. It just wasn't there. But last night for an hour and a half — almost two hours — we listened to this pied piper from Madison, Minnesota. And all of us enjoyed it. He was delightful. He was at ease. He didn't get on a literary high horse and orate as some people think they have to do when they recite poetry. He read it to us as if it was our own language spoken at home.

One fall day several years ago, I went to Doon and checked up on my lot in the graveyard and visited with my brother and a cousin, and, then, because I had a dinner date in Sioux Falls, I drove back. If I had been a musician, I would have put it all down as a piece of music — what I was seeing as I was driving. As I was going along, a poem popped up into my head. I pulled over to the roadside, and this is what I put down:

> On the way to Inwood and Canton
> And finally old Sioux Falls,
> My eyes saw symphonies
> In every valley and river bottom,
> Up every draw and up over every hill,
> Each farmstead
> And old strawpile out in the field,
> The sun setting in my eye,
> The earth turning
> A luminous brown against me,
> The evening star high,
> My eyes painting poetry
> Over the faded cornfields,
> My bowels humming
> Marvelous harmonies.

Following his presentation, Frederick Manfred responded to questions from the audience:

Q. Is Siouxland disappearing? Your poem suggests not.
A. No.

Q. But does it exist for the young people?
A. I think so. In my hometown, many of the bright boys and girls are staying in Luverne. They're not necessarily going off to Minneapolis, New York, or the West Coast. A few of them are still going, but not like in the old days. I've counted 187 college graduates living in the town of Luverne. That's not counting people on the farms. Many of them are my friends: lawyers, teachers, ministers, druggists, and so on. I think more of them are staying around here than in the old days. I believe that if they don't all stay here, it improves the West Coast and the East Coast. Ha, they can use fresh blood.

Q. You talk about the advantages of new kinds of media and technologies. Do you think this, on the other hand, might have stunted people's ability to imagine or to perceive?
A. First off, in the human species, there are not very many bright people, and we may very well destroy ourselves because of it. There are an awful lot of uneducated people, among whom are some bright people who never had a chance to go to school. But below that, there's another level of people who don't have much intelligence. They're good people. They go to church. They obey the law. And they do a lot of hard work for us.

I have some two hundred relatives on my mother's side and some two hundred on my father's side, and probably more now because they keep multiplying. This summer I went to a family reunion, and it struck me there were only four people there that I could talk to who knew what I was doing. The rest had only a vague notion of what I was up to as a writer. But I love them all. Part of my blood runs in their veins.

But at least they have television to look at, which they never had before. In the ancient days, in the days of the scop, every evening after a day's work or a fight or a battle or an excursion somewhere, when people sat around the fire in the evening, the scop would sing. Even the stupid warrior heard it and enjoyed it. And this is what the television set has given most people, a kind of mechanical scop. I prefer a living one, but, at least they've got that. They have a little amusement. And what's the harm in it? It'll keep people out of trouble, too, I think.

I don't believe much in I.Q. tests. They only measure what the guy puts into them. But even if I.Q. tests are 15% off, let's say, for every person who has an I.Q. of 110 there's one with 90, if 100 is the average, you see. And for one with 120, there's a guy down there at 80. Now you have to keep the dull in line somehow, so we have religion for that. And to amuse them we give them TV. But, if you have brains, you don't look at that stuff, except when the Cubs are on.

Q. What is the most interesting thing you've run into in the last ten years?

A. Quantum mechanics, which is some of the most elegant poetry ever invented. The further you go down into the atom, the less mass there is. The final building block of our universe has probably no mass. It's an electric idea, an idea with electricity in it. I hate to use that word *idea* because it right away brings you over into Plato. But in a sense he was on the right track. If you get enough ideas piled up in one spot, a shadow shows up; and if you have enough shadows, you get a slight edge of mass. This suggests that the universe is really made up of particles which do not have any mass. And that to me is one of the most cogent arguments for the fact that there is evidence of God in his real flesh, if you could use *flesh* in that sense. So not only can you believe in God theologically, by way of faith, you can now believe in God by way of examining the inside of an atom. That, to me, has been an absolutely marvelous discovery.

The German Language on the Great Plains

PAUL SCHACH

Paul Schach, an authority on medieval literature and Germanic philology, is Charles J. Mach Professor of Germanic Languages at the University of Nebraska-Lincoln. This lecture was delivered at the 1985 Humanities Seminar at Augustana College.

In 1953 Einar Haugen published his exemplary study of the Norwegian language in America. The second, revised edition of this monograph (1966) is a volume of seven hundred pages. Ever since the appearance of this fascinating book, colleagues have been urging me to do a similar study of the German language in America. The vastness of such an undertaking, even by a team of trained dialectologists, can be seen from the following statistics. Between 1836 and 1930 approximately 810,000 Norwegians immigrated to the United States, of whom about 750,000 remained here. At that time — 1930 — about 750,000 Americans still spoke the Pennsylvania-German dialect as their native tongue. Between 1820 and 1970 over 8,500,000 German-speaking people migrated to the United States. In 1910 the number of Americans who spoke German as their native language was about 9,000,000. In 1894 the number of German-language newspapers in this country exceeded eight hundred. Furthermore, the Norwegian immigrants settled mostly in Wisconsin and the Dakotas. German speakers are found in all forty-eight contiguous states as well as in Alaska and Hawaii, to say nothing about

Canada. To complicate matters even more, speakers of German came from not one country, but from Austria, Switzerland, Alsace, Lorraine, Luxemburg, Denmark, Russia and other eastern European countries, as well as from the many kingdoms, duchies, and principalities that in 1871 were united to form Germany. A further complication is the fact that these speakers of German in America — 9,000,000 of them in 1910, including some of us and the parents of many of us — did not speak a single, unified language, but dozens and dozens of discrete dialects of two distinct but closely related languages: Low German, spoken in the northern third of Germany, and High German, spoken in central and southern Germany, Alsace, Lorraine, Austria, and Switzerland. These few statistics should suffice, I think, to substantiate my contention that a study of the German language in the United States comparable to that of Haugen's Norwegian study would fill not one such volume but ten.

Part of our task at the outset will be to clarify some *termini technici* or technical terminology. To begin with, the term *dialect* does not have a pejorative connotation for the linguist. A dialect is not a debased, corrupted form of the standard language. Dialect means simply a speech variety. As used in describing the German language, dialect usually means the speech variety of a village or of a small region or geographical area. Even today there are individuals in Europe who speak only their local dialect or *Mundart.* When individuals from several or many villages have to communicate with each other — at school, at work, etc. — a form of superregional speech develops that we call *Umgangssprache,* i.e., supperregional vernacular. Thus a Swabian might say to a friend or relative in his home village: *Noi, i ben eta dort gewea* for *Nein, ich war nicht dort.* But to a stranger from another village he would perhaps say: *Noi, ich ben net dort geweese.* The former is local or regional dialect *(Mundart),* the latter is superregional vernacular or *Umgangssprache.* In Switzerland, Austria, and southern Germany many people today speak both *Mundart* and *Umgangssprache,* but there are others who speak only dialect (mostly older people) and some who speak only superregional vernacular (mostly younger people). Eventually, as more and more individuals study and

90

work outside their native villages, the local dialects will disappear and be replaced by the superregional vernaculars. Language is constantly changing, but the rate of change is not constant, as we shall see presently. A dialect then is not a debased or incorrect form of the standard language, but a perfectly good, and respectable, albeit geographically restricted, form of speech. Dialect, Goethe said, "ist die Sprache der Seele."

The terms that cause the greatest difficulty for the layman are *High German* and *Low German*. The reason for this difficulty is the fact that the layman or nonlinguist insists on misinterpreting these technical terms. For the layman *low* means "inferior," and *high* means "superior." Therefore Low German is bad German and High German is good or correct German. This, of course, is utter and complete *Unsinn,* and yet these misinterpretations persist.

The term *Low German* is a translation of *Niederdeutsch,* a general term designating the dialects of the Low Countries—that is, Belgium and the Netherlands—and of northern Germany. In the broadest sense of the word, English is also a form of *Niederdeutsch.* Popularly, the varieties of *Niederdeutsch* spoken in Germany—as opposed to English and those dialects spoken in the Lowlands—are called *Plattdeutsch. Plattdeutsch* means "flat" or "even" German. From the adjective *platt,* "flat, even," is derived the verb *plätten* "to flatten, to make even." In northern Germany *plätten* is used instead of *bügeln* in the sense of "to iron." Some of you, I am sure, use *plätten* in this sense. In my Palatine dialect we say *biggele. Hait muss ich wäsche un marriche muss ich biggele.* In Sutton, Nebraska, and in many places in the Dakotas and Canada you can hear this kind of *Pfälzisch* or Palatine German spoken still today. But we must return to our discussion of *Hochdeutsch* and *Plattdeutsch.*

Despite the fact that the meanings of *Hochdeutsch, Niederdeutsch,* and *Plattdeutsch* are perfectly clear and obvious, many individuals, as already stated, perversely insist on misinterpreting these terms. Their circular reasoning runs like this. *Hochdeutsch*—by which they mean the standard written language, that is, *Schriftdeutsch*—is "good" German. Therefore *Plattdeutsch,* which they misinterpret as "low" German, must be a debased, "incorrect" form of German. And since all dialects, they believe, are "low" German, it follows logically that they must also be debased or incorrect forms of language. Throughout the Great Plains I have repeatedly been told by speakers of Russian-German dialects that they have no real language. "What we speak," they say, "is merely a *lingo*. It's not a real language." Who taught these good people such utter *Unsinn?* Teachers and clergymen, all of whom should have known better. Let me give you a few examples of this misguided concern on the part of teachers that their students should always speak correct, "high" German from my own experience. In high school, I usually spoke dialect with certain friends. One day a teacher approached us and admonished us to speak English. One of our group boldy retorted, "Ich schwätz daitsch wann ich daitsch schwätze will." "Then at least speak correct High German and not that awful Low German *Kauderwelsch!*" When the teacher had disappeared around the corner, the young man muttered, "Ich schwätz wie mer der Schnawwel gewachse is!" As a freshman in college I habitually spoke dialect with an Alsatian student. Whenever our German professor overheard us, she snorted "Küchendeutsch!" My mother, who had been thoroughly indoctrinated as a child, passed on the misinformation to me: "Mir schwätze Hessisch," she declared, "un des is Blattdaitsch!" After studying the history of the German language and German dialectology for several years, I ventured to correct my mother's linguistic misapprehensions. "Was mir schwätze," I explained, "die Sprooch is Pälzisch, und Pälzisch is Hochdaitsch." My intentions were good, but my pedagogical endeavor was not overly successful. "Schwätz mer doch net so dumm, du glee Spitzbiewle," was her admonition. As an afterthought she added: "Die gelärnde Brotfresser wisse aa net alles." Some of you have probably had similar experiences.

Now that we have agreed on the meaning of the technical vocabulary, we must ask ourselves what aspects of German in America can be dealt with most meaningfully within the context of this brief essay. One such aspect is "German as a foreign language, as a subject to be learned in school." One entire volume of our ten-volume *German Language in America* could be devoted to this topic.

You may be surprised to learn that in the early 1800s a veritable "German mania" broke out in — of all places — xenophobic New England. One of the most influential pioneers of this enthusiasm for the German language and German literature was John Quincy Adams. Adams began his study of German in 1782 at the age of fourteen, when he served as French interpreter to the American ambassador to the court of Catherine the Great. Fourteen years later, in the Netherlands, he witnessed a performance of the opera *Oberon,* based on the poem by Wieland. Shortly afterward he was appointed ambassador to the Prussian court in Berlin. Here he resumed his study of German and translated various literary works into English. Among these was Wieland's *Oberon,* which he completed in 1801. Thus the sixth president of the United States was one of the first Americans to learn to appreciate the importance of German literature and the German language.

The German mania in New England was infectious. Soon New Englanders began to study in Germany — especially at the universities of Göttingen and Heidelberg. Probably the best known of these American students to most of us is the poet and Harvard professor of modern languages Henry Wadsworth Longfellow. Not only did Longfellow teach the German language and German literature at Harvard; like John Quincy Adams, he also made English translations of German poems. Probably most of us have read his English version of Goethe's second "Wanderers Nachtlied," or "The Evening Song of the Wanderer." The original is as follows:

> Über allen Gipfeln
> Ist Ruh,
> In allen Wipfeln
> Spürest du
> Kaum einen Hauch,
> Die Vögelein schweigen im Walde,
> Warte nur, balde
> Ruhest du auch.

Longfellow's translation retains the simple imagery:

O'er all the hill-tops
Is quiet now,
In all the tree-tops
Hearest thou
Hardly a breath;
The birds are asleep in the trees;
Wait: soon like these
Thou too shalt rest.

Two interpretations are possible: these could be the words of a weary traveler looking forward to a good night's sleep following hours of trudging roads and streets—possibly a journeyman in search of work. Or the images can be interpreted symbolically as the yearning of a weary pilgrim "within a foreign land" for eternal rest. As we grow older, the second, symbolical interpretation perhaps becomes more attractive and appealing to us.

Of all the many German enthusiasts in New England, probably Ralph Waldo Emerson had the most accurate and profound understanding of contemporary German literature and philosophy. Emerson once said of his Concord group that Goethe "was the cow from which all their milk was drawn." The metaphor may be inelegant, but it probably is correct. As Emerson perceptively remarked, it was not the English who did the thinking for Europe, but the Germans. John Quincy Adams, Henry Wadsworth Longfellow, and Ralph Waldo Emerson deserve to be studied more thoroughly by teachers and students of early American literature. Unfortunately, some students of early American literature seem to be only faintly aware of its German roots.

For over a century German played an important role in American schools: as the medium or vehicle of instruction in parochial and even some public schools and as a subject to be studied by pupils. Again let me quote just a few statistics. In 1915 fully 25% of all high school pupils in America were enrolled in German-language courses. In Nebraska in 1913 German was taught in 150 schools, and in 1915 German instruction was given in 222 schools in this state. In Omaha 3,500 pupils learned German in fifteen elementary schools, and in Lincoln German was taught in five elementary schools, one of which had few if any pupils of German background. With the entry of the United States into World War I — remember the *Lusitania!* — this situation changed abruptly.

Another approach to an understanding of the significance of the German language in America and especially on the Great Plains is provided by a perusal of German-language newspapers. In 1840 there were approximately forty German newspapers in the United States. In 1876 there were seventy-four dailies and 374 weeklies. By 1894 the total number, we recall, exceeded eight hundred. In 1920 there were 278; in 1930, 172; and in 1975 only forty-four German-language periodicals were published in this country. In this area the most influential papers were the *Dakota Freie Presse* (1874-1954), the *Lincoln Freie Presse* (founded 1884), and the *Omaha Tägliche Tribüne,* which outlasted World Word I and World War II.

What were and are the functions of such newspapers? For most immigrants ethnic newspapers are the major source or almost the only source of information about the strange new world in which they suddenly find themselves — information about laws and customs, climate and crops, rights and duties, political issues, and naturalization procedures.

Conversely, these newspapers provided information about the immigrants' European homelands as well as fiction and poetry in the mother tongue — often quite sentimental — as a sort of *Ersatz* for the homeland during the long and difficult period of acculturation. It is not an exaggeration to assert that many German farmers, merchants, and artisans on the Great Plains were far better informed about European affairs around 1900 than some of us are today — thanks largely to their German-language newspapers. This was especially true of readers of the *Dakota Freie Presse,* which was a truly international newspaper. Its columns provided individuals along the Volga and especially in South Russia as well as in North and South America the opportunity to keep in close contact with each other for years. Both of these functions eased and accelerated the transition from being Germans to becoming German-Americans. Paradoxically, the more efficiently the ethnic newspapers performed these functions, the sooner they went out of business.

Carl Schurz emphasized still another function of the German-language press. These newspapers promoted cooperation among Germans living in the United States and Canada by giving them a sense of identity, community, and cohesion. The Catholic Luxemburgers, the Black Sea Mennonites and Calvinists, and the Volga-German and Low-German Lutherans had little in common in regard to religious affiliation, dialect, or national origin. But individuals from all of these diverse groups read the *Lincoln Freie Presse,* which in 1905 had over 158,000 subscribers, or the *Dakota Freie Presse,* or the *Omaha Tägliche Tribüne.* And these and other German-language newspapers helped the immigrants to clarify their perceptions of themselves as German-Americans and as citizens or future citizens of their new homeland.

Still another function of German-language newspapers, which is sometimes overlooked, is the use of such publications to advertise the availability of land at reasonable prices. It has been asserted that Charles Sealsfield's popular novel about Texas, *The Cabin Book,* was more influential than any other single event or effort in bringing Germans to that state. But there must also be a causal relationship between the establishment of the *Galveston Zeitung* in 1846 and the fact that by 1850 Germans comprised about 20% of the white population of Texas.

The earliest German-language newspaper to be established in Nebraska was the *Nebraska Deutsche Zeitung,* the first issue of which appeared at Nebraska City on 4 April 1861. The founder and editor was Dr. Friedrich Renner, a physician from Speyer who had received his medical degree at the University of Paris. The primary purpose of the *Deutsche Zeitung,* Dr. Renner declared, was "to circulate everywhere the glad tidings of a new extensive territory where the best land under the sun could be had for the government price of $1.25 an acre" and where there were good opportunities for employment for those who did not want to acquire land. Renner mailed 150 copies of each issue of his newspaper to Germany, Austria, and the provinces of Alsace and Lorraine.

Some newspapers were even more actively involved in attracting German settlers to the Great Plains. The *Dakota Freie Presse,* for example, from time to time had reporters in Germany as well as in Russia. O. F. Davis, who published *Der Pionier* in Omaha, was a land commissioner for the Union Pacific Railroad. *Der Nebraska Ansiedler,* which was edited in Lincoln, Nebraska, but issued by the Mennonite Publishing Company at Elkhorn, Indiana, was subsidized by the Burlington and Missouri Railroad. These two railroad companies had 7,200,000 acres of land to sell. And Friedrich Hedde, to cite just one more example, served as an immigrant agent in Germany for the state of Nebraska before founding the *Anti-Monopolist* in Grand Island.

Among the interesting features of German-language newspapers were poems, occasional pieces, or even regular columns in dialect rather than in standard German. The *Weltblatt,* founded at Grand Island, Nebraska, was the only newspaper published entirely in Low German. As the number of German readers decreased from natural attrition, newspaper editors hit upon the idea of publishing bilingual papers, none of which was very successful. Both English and German readers objected to paying full price for half a newspaper! *Die Staatspresse* (originally the *Dakota Staatszeitung*) was unique in that it was trilingual, Norwegian being added as the third language.

The history of German-language newspapers in America remains to be studied. Karl Wittke has written a useful book on the subject, and Karl Arndt and Mary E. Olson have provided a good working bibliography and miscellaneous statistical information. But a scholarly presentation of the importance of German-language newspaper publication in the United States and Canada is a task that will, I hope, become more attractive to younger scholars as interest in historical German-Americana continues to grow. Such newspapers as have been preserved will help us German-Americans to answer the questions: Who are we? What are our roots? Where did we come from? What are our unique contributions to America? And the examination of these and other ethnic newspapers, until recently studiously ignored by historians, may well tell us a story about America significantly different from the *Dichtung und Wahrheit* we learned from our schoolbooks.

Years ago Hermann Raster, editor of Chicago's *Illinois Staatszeitung,* asserted that the German press in America was quite as important for German-Americans as were their German churches and German schools. I am not quite sure how one would go about measuring the relative importance of these three institutions for the preservation of the German language. Certainly German newspapers helped the immigrants to preserve their native language along with their sanity, but second-generation German-Americans seldom read German newspapers. Unless there is a sufficient flow of immigrants into a community, ethnic newspapers are usually at best a one-generation enterprise. What about religion and language? We often hear it said that "religion preserves language and language preserves religion." I once believed that myself, and there is some evidence to support that belief. There still exist Amish communities in this country in which the older generation speaks Pennsylvania German and in which religious services are conducted in a form of *Bibeldeutsch*. More than 20,000 Hutterites in Canada and the Dakotas have been able to preserve their Bavarian dialect for three generations in their communes. But it takes more than religion to preserve an ethnic language in a country that is basically hostile to "foreigners." It requires sufficient isolation, ethnic homogeneity, and "critical mass" to preserve German religious services for more than two — or at the utmost three — generations.

Mennonite and Calvinist communities, such as those at Henderson and Sutton, Nebraska, Pretty Prairie and Moundridge, Kansas, and Freeman, South Dakota, have been able to retain their ancestral dialects for three generations and their German church services for two generations. Indeed, in one Sutton Reformed Church, religious services are conducted exclusively in German even today. Each of these South-Russian German communities was blessed with the requisite degree of homogeneity, isolation, and exclusiveness necessary for language retention. By contrast, the loss of the ancestral dialect and the transition from German to English among most Volga Germans — especially those who immigrated in the 1920s — occurred with almost incredible rapidity. In the first place, the essential "critical mass" and the other requisites already mentioned were usually lacking among the Volga Germans. And in the second place, the very strategies that helped preserve German culture in Russia — language and religion —

backfired in this land of high technology, rapid mobility, and mass culture. Here religion did not preserve language. On the contrary, churches had to make a quick transition from German to English in order to retain their second-generation membership. All of us—or at least most of us—have heard or read stories about this language gap and language transition in churches from several points of view.

And now we finally come to the aspect of the study of German that is most fascinating to me as a linguist: the study of dialects. Here we can observe at close range forms of language change that took place, say, in English during a period of well over a thousand years. When we compare *Beowulf,* Chaucer's *Canterbury Tales,* Shakespeare's *Hamlet* or the King James version of the Bible, we can scarely believe that we are dealing with one and the same language. Just as English changed under the impact of Latin, Danish, Norman and Central French, for example, German dialects have changed under the impact of Standard German, other dialects, Russian (for some) and English.

Let us first of all make a brief comparison between certain aspects of the history of the English language and the development of a Russian-German dialect. Shortly after the Romans withdrew from Britain (ca. 410), three Low-German-speaking tribes, the Jutes, the Saxons, and the Angles, established themselves and their dialects there. The country came to be known as England. The dialects they spoke are popularly called Anglo-Saxon, although Old English is preferred by philologists. From Roman merchants, before the migration from Germany, the English acquired words like *street, inch, pound, cheese,* and *kitchen.* With the introduction of Christianity more Latin (and some Greek) words were added to the vocabulary, such as *angel, noon, psalm, relic, temple,* etc. Several centuries later the Danes invaded and occupied England, and, indeed, Canute the Great ruled the country for a short while (ca. 1015). From the Danes the English acquired such words as *husband, law, egg, take, call,* the pronouns *they, their, them,* and virtually all words beginning with sk-, such as *skill, sky, skull, skirt,* etc. The Norman Conquest (1066) opened the gates to a flood tide of French words. When we consider that since that time English was not used by an English king to address the English parliament until 1399, we are not surprised to find that over half of our vocabulary today is of French derivation. Thus modern English is a language with a Low German structure and basic vocabulary—15% of the words—and a total vocabulary of which 85% of the lexical items are non-English.

A convenient dialect with which to make comparisons is that of Sutton, Nebraska, which is very similar to the dialects spoken in Eureka, South Dakota, Ashley and Dickinson, North Dakota, and various other dialects in the Dakotas and Canada. Shortly after 1800 a number of families from various villages in the Palatinate and adjacent areas of France and Germany migrated to the Ukraine, where they established the villages of Worms, Rohrbach, and Johannestal. In 1874 some of the descendants of the Palatine emigrants immigrated to Nebraska and settled in and around Sutton. At the time of the emigration from the Palatinate, their Palatine dialects contained French words, such as *adjé,* "goodbye," *Bummeránz,* "orange," *Gagummer,* "cucumber," *Sos,* "sauce," and *Spikdákel,* "noise, uproar," etc. In their new homes in South Russia the colonists acquired Slavic words, mostly for things that were new to them and for which their dialects consequently had no designations: *babuschka,* "kerchief," *basaar,* "street market," *holúptsi,* "cabbage rolls," *kvass,* "fermented cereal drink," *verscht,* "unit of distance (⅔ mile)," and *vodka,* "spirits." The total number of Slavic words in the vocabulary of the average Palatine colonist probably did not exceed one hundred before 1870. In America, however, the number of English words that found their way into the ancestral language increased in proportion to the number of technological gadgets that appeared in the kitchen, on the farm, and elsewhere. In Austria, Switzerland, and Germany, dialect speakers must use standard German designations for such things; in America they similarly use English labels for the same objects. As various tests have shown, the number of "foreign" words used by speakers of German dialects in America or abroad can range from ca. 5% to 50% depending on the topic under discussion. A similar situation prevails with Czech, Danish, Norwegian, Swedish, etc.

From this sketchy comparison we can see that the English language and German dialects in America—especially those that have been twice transplanted—have undergone similar and parallel developments in regard to their lexica or vocabularies. Linguistic changes that we can observe in our moribund German dialects are similar to changes that occurred in English far from us in time and space. In this brief survey we considered only lexical items that were acquired almost without change by one language from another. But there are many ways in which languages can influence each other. (And incidentally, the influence of German and other ethnic languages on American English is also significant and interesting to specialist and layman alike.) Especially intriguing are the kinds of influences Leonard Bloomfield called "intimate borrowing." Intimate borrowing includes semantic loans, which come about when a native word in language A acquires a meaning from a homophone or close analogue from language B. Thus German *Acker,* which means "arable field" in Europe, has taken on the meaning of its English cognate *acre* in America. A similar semantic shift has occurred with German *Trubel,* which means "turmoil, confusion" in the old country, but "trouble" in the New World. Here we find one of the main sources for bilingual humor, of both the innocent, unwitting kind as well as of the deliberate, sometimes malicious variety. One volume of our ten-volume work on the *German Language in America* could be devoted to the influence of German and English on each other. One chapter of this book would have to be devoted to both unintentional and intentional bilingual humor.

One of the questions most frequently asked of dialectologists is this: Can you locate the homeland of our people in Germany on the basis of our dialect? The answer to this question is: sometimes, yes; more often, perhaps; and far too often, probably not. The problems are most complex. In general, we have our best luck with Palatine dialects, especially those from South Russia. On linguistic evidence we can locate the origin of the dialect of Sutton, Nebraska, and of various places in the Dakotas and Canada. This *Beheimatung* or *Heimatbestimmung* is substantiated by the fairly good documentary evidence regarding the original homelands of the Black Sea Germans despite the fact that these ancestors spent three generations in the Ukraine before they came to the Great Plains.

The Swabian dialects from the Ukraine are much more difficult to classify, and here we would have little success in locating their exact points of origin. In the case of the Volga-German dialects, too, we would not be very successful except in a few cases. The most striking case is the wonderful dialect of Norka. Over two centuries after the forebears of our Nebraska Norkarer left central Hesse, the American Norka dialect can be located near Büdingen in central Hesse. Generally, however, central Hessian dialects, like Swabian dialects, tend to lose the primary phonological features that are characteristic of their precise German homelands. The dialects of the Amana Germans of Iowa and of the Balzerer in Lincoln and elsewhere should be almost identical with that of the Norkarer, but today they would have to be located about one hundred miles southwest of their actual homeland in Germany if we had to rely entirely on linguistic-dialectal evidence.

The first German settlers on the plains came from the German-speaking areas of western Europe. As we have seen, Texas had a substantial German population as early as 1850, and by 1872, just before the influx of Germans from eastern Europe, the number of German speakers in Nebraska exceeded 55,000. Most of the German dialects still spoken on the Great Plains, however, came by way of Russia, the Ukraine, and other areas of eastern Europe. It will be neccessary to say a few words about this linguistic detour.

During the years 1763-69, 103 German villages with a total population of 23,109 persons were established on the Volga River. These colonists had responded to the invitation of Catherine the Great, who promised them freedom of worship, freedom from military service, and general autonomy within their individual villages. Many of these colonists came from central and southern Hesse, and some of their American descendants still speak Hessian or Rhenish Franconian dialects. Hardships suffered during the Seven Years War (1756-63) were a major motivation for this exodus of German peasants, artisans, and others from their homelands.

During the period 1804-24, a second major emigration from German countries took place. At this time the Russian government attracted several thousand settlers from the Palatinate, Alsace, northern Baden, and Württemberg—areas that had been devastated during the Napoleonic wars—to the Ukraine, where they established colonies near Odessa. These colonists, who had been carefully selected, suffered less hardships than those on the Volga. Some of them came to be wealthy landowners.

The peregrinations of the Mennonites were somewhat more complicated. One group left the Low Countries during the sixteenth century and settled in Prussia, where they gradually replaced their Flemish and Frisian dialects with a Low German dialect. In 1788 migration to South Russia began, where the pacifist Anabaptists were granted privileges similar to those granted other German colonists. They established colonies along the Dnieper and Molotschna Rivers and elsewhere in the Ukraine. A second, smaller group of Mennonites left their homes in Switzerland for the Palatinate in 1670, where they remained until 1787, when they continued on to Volhynia. This group also abandoned its ancestral tongue, Swiss Alemannic, in favor of a north Palatine dialect. The most tortuous path of all was followed by the Hutterian Brethren. Persecution drove them from Moravia and then successively from Slovakia, Transylvania, and Wallachia, until finally, in 1842, they settled in the Ukraine near the Molotschna Mennonites. There were, of course, many other German settlements in eastern Europe, in the Crimea, and beyond the Ural Mountains; but this brief sketch should suffice for our present purpose.

The exodus from Russia was precipitated by the abrogation of the promise of special privileges in 1871. Faced with the loss of religious and linguistic identity, as well as with many years of service in the Russian armed forces, many German colonists prepared to emigrate. The Mennonites had maintained contact with their coreligionists in Prussia and in America, and the colonists on the Volga and in the Ukraine had both recently been visited by Russian Germans currently living in the United States. All three groups sent scouts to the New World, and within a few years substantial immigration to the Great Plains was under way. Yankton, Lincoln, and Russell, Kansas, were three of the major distribution points from which the immigrants proceeded north, west, and south. In 1920 the Russian-German population in the United States was somewhat over 300,000, of whom over one-half resided in North Dakota (69,985), Kansas (31,512), South Dakota (30,937), Nebraska (22,421) and Colorado (21,067). At this time dozens of Low and especially High German dialects were spoken on the Great Plains even though vicious propaganda and punitive legislation during World War I caused many parents not to teach their children their ancestral language.

As already mentioned, the retention of immigrant languages and dialects depends on a number of factors. On the Hutterian *Brüderhöfe,* conditions for dialect use and preservation had been ideal. But the precarious isolation of the communes is being severely endangered by two factors: compulsory public education and farm equipment repair manuals. Whereas the Hutterians use less than fifty foreign loanwords acquired in Europe, their fascinating, archaic Tyrolean-Corinthian dialect is rapidly being inundated with English technical terms. A similar condition obtains in Germany. When farmers in Eastphalia, for example, discuss the use and repair of farm machinery, they constantly shift back and forth between their native Low German and standard German. Dialects simply have no technological terminology. The socio-linguistic assimilation of Hutterites and other German-Americans is a fertile field of study for the linguist and dialectologist.

Another important aspect of German dialectology on the Great Plains is the comparison between a given dialect as spoken here and as spoken in the homeland. Since the original homelands of many German settlers in the Ukraine are known, some of the Black Sea dialects in the Dakotas and in Canada should be investigated from this point of view. Such studies would involve comparisons of the phonology, morphology, syntax, intonation, and vocabulary of the German and the German-American varieties of these dialects.

The most urgent problem facing us at the moment is the need to record on cassettes as much dialect material as possible as soon as possible, for this precious part of our ethnic heritage is rapidly disappearing. Standard questionnaires and word lists have been prepared for this purpose. With the help of dialect dictionaries, maps, and atlases, the recorded materials can quickly be roughly classified. Such recordings can be supplemented by recorded directed or casual conversation (if the interviewer speaks a compatible dialect), by family chronicles, anecdotes, and the like. Many persons still remember proverbs, children's rimes, prayers, etc. from their childhood. And occasionally a storyteller is found who can relate adventures in the old country and on the plains during the early days of immigration and settlement. How can this wealth of folklore, history, and linguistic material be recorded for future study before it disappears forever?

SUGGESTED READINGS

Cultural and Historical Background

Giesinger, Adam. *From Catherine to Khrushchev: The Story of Russia's Germans.* Lincoln: American Historical Society of Germans from Russia, 1974.

Hale, Douglas. *The Germans from Russia in Oklahoma.* Norman: U of Oklahoma P, 1980.

Harding, Anneliese, ed. *John Quincy Adams: Pioneer of German-American Literary Studies.* Boston: Goethe Institute, 1979.

Height, Joseph S. *Memories of the Black Sea Germans: Highlights of Their History and Heritage.* Chelsea, Michigan, 1979.

Koch, Fred C. *The Volga Germans in Russia and the Americas from 1763 to the Present.* University Park and London: Pennsylvania State UP, 1977.

Lich, Glen E. and Dona B. Reeves, eds. *German Culture in Texas: A Free Earth, Essays from the 1978 Southwest Symposium.* Boston: Twayne, 1980.

Luebke, Frederick C. *Bonds of Loyalty: German Americans and World War I.* DeKalb: Northern Illinois UP, 1974.

— — —. *Immigrants and Politics: The Germans of Nebraska, 1880-1900.* Lincoln: U of Nebraska P, 1969.

Olson, Paul, ed. *Broken Hoops and Plains People: A Catalogue of Ethnic Resources in the Humanities: Nebraska and Thereabouts.* Lincoln: Nebraska Curriculum Development Center, 1976.

Rath, George. *The Black Sea Germans in the Dakotas.* Freeman, S.D.: Pine Hill, 1977.

Rife, Janet Warkentin. *Germans and German-Russians in Nebraska.* Lincoln: Center for Great Plains Studies and the Nebraska Curriculum Development Center, 1980.

Rippley, LaVern J. *The German-Americans.* Boston: Twayne, 1976.

Sallet, Richard. *Russian-German Settlements in the United States.* Trans. LaVern J. Rippley and Armand Bauer. Fargo: North Dakota Institute for Regional Studies, 1974.

Schach, Paul. "Russian Wolves in Folktales and Literature of the Plains: A Question of Origins," *Great Plains Quarterly* 3 (1983): 67-78.

Totten, Christine M. *Roots in the Rhineland: America's German Heritage in Three Hundred Years of Immigration, 1683-1983.* New York: German Information Center, 1983.

German-Language Newspapers

Arndt, Karl J. R. and May E. Olson, eds. *German-American Newspapers and Periodicals, 1732-1955.* Heidelberg: Quelle und Meyer, 1961.

Richter, Anton H. " 'Gebt ihr den Vorzug': The German-Language Press of North and South Dakota," *South Dakota History* 10 (1980): 190-209.

Rippley, LaVern J. "A History of the *Dakota Freie Presse,*" *Heritage Review* 7 (1973): 9-18.

Schach, Paul. "German-Language Newspapers in Nebraska, 1860-1890," *Nebraska History* 65 (1984): 84-107.

Wittke, Carl. *The German-Language Press in America.* Lexington: U of Kentucky P, 1957.

Dialectology and Linguistics

Bender, Jan E. "Consonantal Aberrations in Low-German Dialects on the Great Plains," *Selecta: Journal of the Pacific Northwest Council on Foreign Languages* 1 (1980): 130-33.

Buchheit, Robert H. "The Decline of German Settlement Dialects on the Great Plains between the Two World Wars," *Schatzkammer* 8 (1982): 48-71.

Gilbert, Glen G. *The German Language in America: A Symposium.* Austin and London: U of Texas P, 1971.

Keel, William D. "On the Heimatbestimmung of the Ellis County (Kansas) Volga-German Dialects," *Yearbook of German-American Studies* 17 (1982): 99-110.

Rein, Kurt. *Religiöse Minderheiten als Sprachgemeinschaftsmodelle: Deutsche Sprachinseln täuferischen Ursprungs in den Vereinigten Staaten von Amerika.* Wiesbaden: Franz Steiner Verlag, 1977.

Schach, Paul. "Semantic Borrowing in Pennsylvania German," *American Speech* 26 (1951): 257-67.

— — —. "Die Lehnprägungen der pennsylvania-deutschen Mundart," *Zeitschrift für Mundartforschung* 22 (1955): 215-22.

— — —. "Pfälzische Entlehnungen in der amerikanischen Umgangssprache," *Rheinische Vierteljahrsblätter* 20 (1955): 223-37.

— — —. "Zum Lautwandel im Rheinpfälzischen: die Senkung von kurzem Vokal zu *a* vor *r*-Verbindung," *Zeitschrift für Mundartforschung* 26 (1958): 200-22 and 6 maps.

— — —, ed. *Languages in Conflict: Linguistic Acculturation on the Great Plains.* Lincoln and London: U of Nebraska P, 1980.

— — —. "Phonetic Change in German Dialects on the Great Plains," *Yearbook of German-American Studies* 18 (1983): 157-71.

— — —. "Hessian and Palatine Dialects on the Great Plains." *Dialectology, Linguistics, Literature: Festschrift for Carroll E. Reed.* Ed. Wolfgang W. Moelleken. Göppingen: Kümmerle Verlag, 1984, 232-48.

Scheer, Herfried. "The Hutterian German Dialect: A Study in Sociolinguistic Assimilation and Differentiation," *Mennonite Quarterly Review* 54 (1980): 229-43.

Idols of the Tribe, Idols of the Theater: Reporting on Native Americans

RONALD ROBINSON

Ronald Robinson is chairman of the Department of English and Journalism at Augustana College. This address was given at the 1986 Journalism Forum at Augustana College.

Remember *You Are There*? You might if you were old enough to be watching television in the late fifties. The program featured Walter Cronkite — a very young Uncle Walter, before Kennedy was shot, before the *Eagle* landed, before Watergate, before Cronkite became the most trusted man in America — Walter Cronkite pretending to anchor live coverage of great historical events: the death of Socrates, the death of Lincoln, the Trojan War, Custer's Last Stand, and so on. *You Are There* was shown on Sunday, then regarded by the network programmers as a kind of hopeless Low-Ratings Land where educational and religious shows fought listless battles for a share of a pathetically small audience. The show was a pastiche of the kind of history teaching in which the teacher puts on a Roman toga and masquerades as Caesar and pseudo-journalism in the tradition of Orson Welles' *War of the Worlds*. It was quite entertaining, sometimes even moving, sometimes unintentionally comic when the central anachronism grew painfully obvious: reporters in double-breasted suits thrusting microphones into the face of a costumed actor, usually Shepherd Strudwick, to inquire in urgent tones about how the Civil War might turn out or whether Socrates might wise up and beat it before his execution. Since it was all scripted, some of the tastelessness of real-life journalism was avoided. No one asked, "How do you feel about your husband dying, Mrs. Lincoln?" For members of the generation that cut its teeth on television back then, part of the shock and surrealism of the Kennedy assassination had to derive from a strange sense of deja vu. There was Walter Cronkite again, using the same familiar, reassuring tones, the same live reports, the same kind of impromptu interview, and telling of the death of a revered leader. Except this time it was all, well, unbelievable. Less believable than staged history. *You Are There.* Now you really were there. And you couldn't believe it was happening, even when you saw it with your own eyes, again and again and again.

Journalism as theater, or theater as journalism, that is the inheritance of the electronic media. Today we are all familiar with the theatrics of television reporting. It is a tired old truism that *60 Minutes* is more a show than it is news. You can't rerun news. And the news doesn't take time out for a few minutes with such affable entertainers as Andy Rooney, not often at least. Yet that is where *our* Dan Rather came from, just as Cronkite came from *You Are There.* They both graduated from theater-as-journalism on Sunday to journalism-as-theater five nights a week. Now we all know about media events, photo opportunities, press conferences, and other devices used by those actors or aspiring actors on the national scene to get their faces on the nightly news. Is it really just fate or coincidence that an actor is in the White House? Is it without significance that actors like David Hartman can slide so easily into the role of reporter-anchor? Or that media personalities slip so easily into the role of politician? When Hollywood gets around to filming the life of Ronald Reagan — and we all know they will get around to it — they'll have to get someone younger for the first part of the film: Dutch Reagan as a sports announcer, Ronnie Reagan, matinee idol. David Hartman would be a good choice for Reagan the actors' union boss, Reagan the company spokesman, Reagan the host for *Death Valley Days,* Reagan the voice of conservatism.

But once you got to the White House years, there's only one man who could play the part — Reagan himself. The thought is a little staggering, isn't it? The actor as politician as president playing the role of actor as politician as president. And visiting the set, no doubt, will be fascinated representatives of the media: Mary Hart of *Entertainment Tonight* and Tom Brokaw of *NBC Nightly News,* possibly. And they'll be there not only to report, but to learn. It used to be you went to law school if you had political ambitions. Now you might as well go to Yale Drama School, or Brown Institute.

All this has quite a lot to do with the way the media report on "others." In South Dakota, particularly, we have seen how a dramatic event, a courthouse protest or the seige of a historic site on the reservation, staged or spontaneous, might capture the attention of national media. We have seen how Russell Means, eminently photogenic, the very picture of what an Indian should look like according to Hollywood and media standards, was able to establish himself as a spokesman for Indians in the eyes of the national press, saying his lines clearly, loudly, dramatically, and quotably. Here is Peter Matthiessen's description of Means from *In the Spirit of Crazy Horse:*

> A former rodeo rider and Indian dancer, he wore traditional long braids and bone neck choker, red wind band, black shirt, and embroidered vest, together with a beaded belt and turquoise jewelry, jeans, and boots; in this outfit, he looked like a modern version of the tall and striking Lakota leaders of the nineteenth century, which made him all the more effective as a symbol. Like Dennis Banks, he was eloquent and charismatic, with an instinct for inflammatory statements, and "Banks and Means" were soon synonymous with the AIM cause all around the country. (Matthiessen 38-39)

Make no mistake about it, those days in the early seventies were glory days for the American Indian Movement and to a large extent for the Lakota and other tribes as well. Say what you will about AIM, it accomplished one important thing with the media: it got their attention. And that is no small task.

Compare the farm problem. Five years ago Jeff Greenfield, then a political commentator with CBS News, visited Sioux Falls to take part in a journalism forum. He inquired of the local affiliate about the farm economy and urged it to expand its coverage of the story. At that time the loan default rate was at something like 5%, a figure that bankers and FMHA officials were tossing off as evidence that there was no crisis. Yet even that figure, if properly dramatized, could have got some attention: imagine a small community of perhaps a thousand families in which 5%, or fifty families, were thrown out of their homes and out of their jobs because they couldn't pay the mortgage. Such a situation would surely be regarded as a catastrophe by that small town, and everyone would have paid attention. Yet because the situation at that time was not dramatized, because the farmers who were losing their farms were scattered across the countryside, because it was hard to believe that it could be happening in the midst of the Reagan prosperity, the collapse of the farm economy went largely unnoticed nationally. Five years later, CBS and Dan Rather were in Sioux Falls making much of the farm problem, now elevated to the farm crisis, the plight of the farmers. Was it mere coincidence that in the intervening years two major motion pictures and a marathon music concert and telethon dramatized the farm problem in a way that the media otherwise had not?

The dramatization of Indian concerns was a major accomplishment for AIM, and one for which they must be credited. Most of those concerns, after all, were a good deal older than the farm problem and had been ignored a good deal longer. But those glory days are now a decade distant. Meanwhile, the American Indian Movement seems to have lost momentum and appeal for many Native Americans. Meanwhile, the concerns of the Indians have remained or have increased. Meanwhile, much news on the reservation has gone unreported by the national media, many stories have gone untold, undramatized.

This address is not at all intended as a wholesale condemnation of the press in its coverage of Indian affairs. I feel I must make this disclaimer at the outset because I know a few people in the media who are put on the defensive by any suggestion that there might be some improvement in reporting on Native Americans. They point out the superior reporting that has been done, and they attribute any shortcomings to the lack of Native Americans in the newsroom, or the inability of the Indian to "get his act together." (That last phrase is particularly suggestive, isn't it? "Get his *act* together." As if it is up to the victims of neglect to dramatize how they have been made victims.) But they are right, of course, to some extent. Some excellent reporting has been done. In recent years the Sioux Falls *Argus Leader* has been exemplary in its special features and series on various aspects of Indian life, as well as in its day-to-day coverage. The paper goes out of its way to provide full and fair reporting. It has established a panel of advisers on Indian affairs, and I'm sure it would willingly put one or two Native Americans on its reporting staff, if such reporters were readily available. South Dakota Public Television, as well, has had many informative programs and series on Indian concerns. And the *Argus Leader* and Public Television are not alone—there has been a notable improvement in reporting on Native Americans across the state.

Neither do I see any particular ill will or ill intention toward Indians by the press in general or by the South Dakota press in particular. Quite the contrary. The media appear to be for the most part wholly sympathetic toward Native Americans and sensitive to many of the issues particularly affecting Native Americans. The civil rights movement of past decades has made most citizens more aware of minorities and willing, even eager, to help. And the press has been, if anything, even more affected by such influences. The time is long past when any hint of bigotry would go unchallenged by editors or reporters. Like the rest of us, they want to do right by all minorities, and they bend over backward to do so.

So, if all of that is true—and I think it is—why this speech? For that matter, why this conference?

Those of you who have participated in other sessions of the conference should know the answer to that by now. It is because some Indian stereotypes still prevail. It is because, for all their good intentions, the media can still get it wrong, as Tim Giago frequently points out in his columns. It is because there are not enough Indian journalists to go around, so that reporting and editing is still dominated by a non-Indian point of view. It is because some things can be done to further improve reporting on Native Americans even under these circumstances.

I see two groups of attitudes that particularly affect even the well-intentioned reporter. They are what I will call, following the lead of Sir Francis Bacon, the idols of the tribe and the idols of the theater. In addition to being one of the foremost prose stylists in the English language, Bacon was one of the earliest spokesmen for the scientific approach to understanding. Bacon believed that our understanding is flawed by what he called idols: misperceptions and misconceptions that are either built-in or that obstruct us externally. For example, Bacon is among the first to demonstrate that the very words that we rely upon to convey our thoughts may ironically limit and even corrupt our thinking. The idols of the market-place, he called them. Today we call the study of such error semantics. Indeed, we might at this point get involved in such "empty controversies" as Bacon warned against by questioning the term "Indian" or "Native American" or even "Sioux." Isn't anyone born in America a native American? That would include Bruce Springsteen, surely, along with most of the people in this hall. Should Indians forever be mislabeled because Columbus thought he was going to India? Isn't "Sioux" a derogatory term used only by enemy tribes? As fascinating and even relevant as these questions might be, they are productive only if in the end we agree that when we use a certain word we mean a certain thing and no less and no more. The idols of the cave were for Bacon those flaws in understanding that derived from each individual's limitations. A metaphor for this kind of misperception might be the common experience of looking into a microscope to see an amoeba or paramecium and being able to see only the reflection of your own eyeball. The Greek belief was that man was the measure for all things. But an individual man—shorter, taller, slimmer, fatter, with or without 20-20 vision, with good or bad taste—an individual man can be an unreliable yardstick. Bacon believed

113

that the truer measure, though perhaps less accessible, was not man, but nature. It is against nature that everything, man included, is to be compared. The idea behind all of Bacon's thinking on this subject is that there is a universe out there that few of us see or understand, either because of a failure of vision or because of blinders that we are obliged to wear.

The two categories with which we are especially concerned are the idols of the tribe, those misconceptions and misperceptions that derive from human nature, and the idols of the theater, those errors that are imposed by systems of philosophy. The idols of the tribe include those aspects of European thought that may lead us astray in dealing with "others." And among the idols of the theater are those principles of journalism that may ironically lead reporters into error. Call them idols of the profession, if that will help, but remember that, as I have pointed out earlier, the profession is largely theater.

We have heard a lot of talk, and seen some handwringing in the past few days about images, the images of the Indian in particular, and the impression has been that those images go back to the first contacts between Europeans and Indians. Here's some news for you—they go back a good deal farther than that. Over two thousand years farther back.

In the literature of the Western tradition, the very earliest writing contains reports of "others" that is perhaps representative of the reporting from that time on. Here is an account of such outlanders by a soldier-statesman turned first-person reporter:

[They are] giants, louts, without a law to bless them.
In ignorance leaving the fruitage of the earth in mystery
to the immortal gods, they neither plow nor sow by hand,
nor till the ground, though grain—wild wheat and barley—
grows untended, and wine-grapes, in clusters, ripen in
heaven's rain. [They] have no muster and no meeting,
no consultation or old tribal ways, but each one dwells
in his own mountain cave dealing out rough justice to
wife and child, indifferent to what the others do. (Homer
1:254)

What bothered the reporter about this strange people, about these others, is that they had none of the appurtenances of civilization as he knew it: agriculture, parliaments, traditions, laws. When he attempted to invoke the code of hospitality, known everywhere among civilized men, this people behaved most inhospitably. Moreover, they looked funny. Besides being giants, they each had only one eye, which is what gave them their name — the Cyclopes. And he had it on very direct evidence that they were cannibals. Imprisoned by one of their number and threatened with death, the reporter felt no particular regret about getting the barbarian drunk, tricking him, making him look foolish with his neighbors, and escaping. The reporter's exploits, in fact, sound very similar to some of the accounts I read as a child, in a book that had belonged to my grandfather, called *Pioneer Heroes and Their Daring Deeds.* As he made his get-away, the reporter shouted out his name, address, and zip code, just in case the monster wanted to know where to reach him:

> . . . if ever mortal man inquire how you were put to shame and blinded, tell him Odysseus, raider of cities, took your eye: Laërtes' son, whose home's on Ithaka!
> (Homer 1:264)

Bad luck for Odysseus, Cyclops turned out to be the son of a rather influential god, the god of earthquake, Poseidon, who gave Odysseus no end of grief on the rest of his journey.

Nearly all of the non-Greeks encountered by Odysseus have a mark or two against them: they are cannibals, like the Cicones; or dopers, like the Lotus-Eaters; or outright, all-around barbarians, like the Cyclopes. In his travels and in his reporting on others, Odysseus sets a pattern widely imitated throughout the Western tradition.

Travelers during the late fifteenth and sixteenth centuries reported information just as fantastic as any conveyed by Odysseus. They described men whose faces were where their navels should be, pygmies, giants, one-legged and one-eyed races, and, of course, cannibals. Even the Iberian invaders of Central and South America recorded — in addition to cities and cultures that outshone anything they had known in Europe — barbarous behavior, human sacrifice, and, of course, cannibalism.

Cannibalism serves as well as anything to represent the kind of barbarianism that appalled Europeans who ventured to other continents. From the time of the Greeks onward, it was the most horrible crime that could be imagined. Kronos ate his children and was overthrown and exiled as a result. Tantalus won his most exquisite punishment in the underworld for having enticed the gods to partake in cannibalism. Thyestes tricked Atreus into eating his own child, triggering a tragic chain of events that plagued the house of Atreus from then on. Fictional accounts such as Defoe's *Robinson Crusoe* used the threat of cannibalism as part of the plot structure. The anthropologist Margaret Mead found cannibalism in New Guinea. The missionary in the iron pot has been a standard cartoon gag for decades. It is assumed that the Neanderthals were cannibals, and the Aztecs, and the tribes of Africa. The only trouble with all of this discussion of cannibalism, both factual and fictional, is that the latest research suggests that cannibalism as an accepted custom is a myth. William Arens, a professor of anthropology at the State University of New York at Stony Brook, in his book *The Man-Eating Myth,* says the bloody stories derive from one culture's "negative evaluation of another" (Arens 183).

The Greeks gave us the idea of barbarianism and the word for it: *barbaros.* Anyone who was not Greek was *barbaros,* barbarous, a barbarian. In its most innocuous form, the word meant simply foreigner, but as it came to be used, it carried overtones of rude, uncivilized behavior. The Greeks gave the word to the Romans and the Romans gave it to the French and the French gave it to us, like a disease. And when we caught it, we applied it to the Indians, blacks, Chinese — anyone who was not us. It became one of the idols of the tribe, the idea that anyone outside the tribe was not civilized and therefore not worthy of civilized treatment. If they had no laws, then the laws that applied to us did not apply to them. If they did not share our traditions, then we would not extend our traditions — of civility, of hospitality — to them.

116

Consider the South before the Civil War. The colonnades, the gallantry, the hospitality, all seemed part of a conscious imitation of ancient Greece. Even the slaves — well, the Greeks had slaves. And the black slaves were obviously barbarian. Civilization didn't apply to them, nor gallantry, nor hospitality.

Still, the blacks fared better than the Indians in a number of respects. Isolated from their roots, the blacks adapted to European values, adopted some of them, made use of effective tactics to secure what gains were made in civil rights over the years. The Indians, fortunately not cut off from their roots, unfortunately seemed, until recently, less effective in stating their case. Part of the reason for this state of affairs is surely that the press, well-meaning as it may be, has not been able to cross the bridge between cultures, has not been able to transcend the idols of the tribe in order to establish the empathy required for effective communication.

Let's look at just a few of the attitudes of Europeans (and Anglo-Europeans in America) which constitute the most stubborn barriers to understanding — the most adamant idols of the tribe: the attitudes toward land, toward time, and toward giving.

First, the attitude toward land. For those in the European tradition, land is something to own, to use. They take quite literally those Biblical injunctions that man should take dominion over the earth. Not only *can* man use land, he is obliged to. It is virtually a sin for him not to. Vine Deloria, Jr., has pointed out that one of the most common excuses for taking over Indian tribal land has been that the Indians have not made use of it (*We Talk, You Listen* 182). In the Anglo view, land that has not been put to use has gone to waste. A television commercial from Archer-Daniels-Midland, currently running, incorporates dramatic pictures of land erosion of the dust bowl days and of the present time, yet it blames this loss of soil, and consequently the loss of farm productivity, not upon land use, land overuse, land misuse — but upon "neglect." Look at the use that land has been put to in America, and what has come of it: mining, housing development, farming, waste disposal, leading to accelerated erosion, contamination, urban blight. Deloria makes it clear: "The white destroyed his land. He destroyed the planet earth" (*We Talk* 186).

For the Indian, on the contrary, European concepts of land ownership or land use are repugnant. Land can no more be owned than air or water, in the Indian view. All those things are there, and they can be enjoyed and even "used" in a sense, by all men, all animals and living things. But no one man or group of men has superior claim to them. Eventually, as the Anglo-Europeans encroached upon Indian hunting grounds, the tribes were persuaded that land could be set aside for the tribes as a whole. The various treaties over the decades of the nineteenth century were about such persuasions. The Indian tribes were promised certain territories — usually those areas perceived by whites as inferior or "waste" land — in return for an end to hostilities. Of course, the land "given" to the Indians was the land that was theirs in the first place. It is much as if I stole a hundred dollars from you and then gave you ten dollars of that amount back to agree that I would not try to steal more, and that you wouldn't call the cops. Thus, the reservation system. But of course, after a while all that "waste" land given to the Indians began to look more attractive, more useable. Gold was discovered on it, say, or oil, or coal, or ranchers started to covet it for range land, or farmers for farm land. So the allotment process, which doled out small portions of the tribal land to individual Indians, was instituted on many reservations. Now the Anglo-European attitude of land ownership was enforced completely, and the result was that reservation lands diminished — bought, swindled, or simply stolen from the individuals (*We Talk* 183). It is easy to see how such policies, more widely instituted, might lead to the disappearance of reservations altogether, which might very well please certain people. Many of us Anglo-Europeans, brought up with our peculiar land ethic, even begrudge the wilderness areas set aside by the govenment through the years. The setting aside of such areas has steadily declined recently, and now is at a complete standstill. Should the trend continue, the relatively few wild places in this country will start to succumb to vacation resorts, oil and gas interests, housing developers, and all of those greedy to get their hands on a few acres or

118

a few hundred thousand acres and to put them to use. Then we will have what we seem most to want, one enormous artificial shopping mall or Astrodome or amusement park — a Disneyland from sea to shining sea.

The Indian attitude toward nature in general is closer to the thinking of the Oriental, Zen or Taoist. These others see the connections between man and nature, not the separation. While volumes have been written in the European tradition to define exactly what it is that separates man from the rest of creation, the Indian and the Taoist accept that there is no real separation. When the Indian speaks of his brothers, he includes his four-footed and winged and hoofed brothers. If this attitude does not entirely absolve these other cultures from blame in man's gradual decimation of the earth, at least it confers upon them credit for knowing what is going on and for perhaps slowing the process.

The European attitude toward time, almost inevitably bound up with attitudes toward work, constitutes another of the idols of the tribe. For us whites, the precise measurement of time is so important that we have worked out innumerable ways of dividing and keeping track of the years, months, days, hours, minutes, seconds, and milliseconds. There's work time, play time, breakfast time, dinner time, and so on. Clocks give us a way of knowing when to get together to do something. Moreover, the clocks and watches and calendars and calendar-watches constantly remind us that time is passing, and that our lives are passing with it. They tell us, ticking on our wrists or on the wall or in our ears, that it's getting late, that if we're going to get something done, it better be done soon, it better be done now. Duty calls. Time to get to work. To live is to work. Forget the chicken-egg arguments over which comes first. To work is to live. If you don't work or if you're late for work or if you'd prefer not to work, you're a lazy bum who doesn't deserve a living. You all know the rules, the rules that govern the way we live. They are the product of the Industrial Revolution, the Protestant Work Ethic, and thousands of other influences going all the way back to the Greeks again. In Greek myth, Kronos was a cruel god. Yes, the same one who ate his children. But he *was* a god. The Indians did not make a god of time.

What should be emphasized is that the Indian attitude toward time is natural, in tune with nature, and deeply engrained in the culture. It does not make the Indian lazy. It does make the Anglo-European culture appear to the Indian frenetic, obsessed with schedules and deadlines, a destroyer of nerves and of bodies. Productivity, that modern catchword and whip for the working person, translates into the greatest amount of work in the least amount of time. Who, outside the bosses and the efficiency experts, really wants that? Everyone knows that the only product worth the effort is the one upon which time and care have been lavished. Journalists, who are constantly challenged to beat the clock, must surely see the justice of such a view. We see the senselessness of a clock-driven society and we would gladly trade it for a gentler, more natural pace, but we are trapped. And if we are trapped, we want everybody trapped. Whatever resentment we have for the Indian views of time and of work are not *in* the views themselves, because they are the views we would gladly endorse. Rather, the resentment comes for the person who acts upon those views and does exactly what we would do if we were not driven to cowardice by peer pressure, boss pressure, and culture pressure.

Giving is another subject about which there is cultural disagreement. In the Western tradition, generosity is certainly a virtue, but it has become institutionalized, impersonalized, and ultimately commercialized. Today we give to fund-raising groups that skim so much off the top as overhead and distribute the rest no doubt fairly, of course deservedly, but certainly impersonally. We seldom know who or what we're really giving to. And our official day of giving, Christmas, is preceded by a day of frantic last minute shopping and followed by a day of frantic refunding and substitution. Our one great day of sharing is an island in a season of greed. The commercialized Christmas as we know it was invented by department stores at the turn of the century. They started at Thanksgiving to remind us of the coming gift day with window displays of Christmas trees and with newspaper advertising featuring a slick modern symbol of giving, Santa

Claus. The almost wholly artificial tradition was passed along by the chain stores, Woolworths and Penneys, and is kept up today by shopping malls the country over. If you work in retail trade you know that the Christmas season is when you make your profit for the year. If you work in the commercial media, you know that the advertising volume during that time is going to pay for baby's shoes and then some. What everybody knows is that it is a hectic time capped by a ritual of gift exchange that seems at times both mechanical and meaningless. You give and worry if the gift is right, you get and pretend to like it even if it's wrong.

The Oglala ceremony of the give-away, by contrast, is personal and touching. Whether the occasion is a death in the family or simply a sense of abundance that calls for sharing, the give-away is an expression of total and absolute generosity. It is giving in the spirit of gratitude and sacrifice. Here is an account from William K. Powers' *Oglala Religion:*

> The give-away associated with the memorial feast is a thanksgiving . . . in which the mourner and his or her family acknowledge the help received from neighbors and kin during the one-year period. A table is set up in the middle of the circular shade or community house and the gifts placed on it. The mourner and close kin stand around the table and select gifts to be given to specific people, whose names are announced by an announcer. As each person's name is called, he or she approaches the table, receives the gift, and shakes hands with all the members of the family. (134)

The mourners' family is often rendered destitute by this ritual, and must rely upon later give-aways to replace basic personal possessions. By comparison, non-Indians don't even know the meaning of "giving till it hurts."

There are many other idols of the tribe that might be discussed. But by now you get the idea. Our culture has certain built-in attitudes which can get in the way of understanding and communication. Ethnocentricities, the sociologist and anthropologists call them. These attitudes affect everyone, not just journalists. All the more reason, therefore, for the journalist to be aware of these cultural obstacles and to attempt to rise above them or at least to acknowledge their existence and to try to pull against the tractor force. We have grown knowledgeable enough now not to expect or demand absolute robotlike objectivity from our correspondents, but we may still ask that they be more widely informed, empathetic, and fair.

That brings us to the second and final category of this brief inventory of pitfalls for the media: the idols of the theater. Or, if you prefer, the idols of the profession. Two widely accepted ideas of what constitutes newsworthiness are timeliness (along with its constant companion, novelty), and prominence.

Certainly one can hardly argue with the concept that what is news is what is new—the latest word, "hot off the press," timely. Yet the present obsession with timeliness is really a rather recent development in journalism, made possible and encouraged by technological development and by competition among news agencies. The early journals in this country and in Europe were of necessity behind the time by days, weeks, even months. It was an accepted condition of publishing that the news could not be timely, so efforts were taken to make it lively and stylish. The kind of journalism practiced by Ben Franklin in the eighteenth century or by Mark Twain in the nineteenth were very much alike, and yet very different from the journalism practiced today. A string of technological wonders—the rotary press, the continuous web press operating at high speed, the linotype machine, offset photolithography, the telegraph, telephone, radio and television, satellite communication—have reduced the lead time between the event and its publication to seconds. Last Sunday, on the news-talk shows, as David Brinkley and others talked with the leaders of opposition to the Marcos regime, they were occasionally put off by an annoying echo of their own words which resulted from the half-second delay of the signal as it was bounced off a satellite. A half-second. That is the lag in information coming from the other side of the world. A half-second from event to publication. No wonder that journalists today are obsessed by timeliness. There is so much happening, here and around the globe, and there is no excuse whatever that the public should not be told what is happening immediately. The spirit of competition, too, acts as a spur for journalists to come up constantly with something new. Competition started back in the previous century as newspapers in New York and Chicago and San Francisco and other metropolitan centers vied for readership, which translated into advertising revenue. And the competition was for the most part healthy, when one paper kept another honest and when all papers had a degree of financial stability that prevented undue pressure from advertisers or other groups. Or it could be unhealthy, as in the case of the newspaper wars which seem to have had a hand in bringing about a real shooting war in Cuba, the Spanish-American War. Today competition between newspapers in the same city is rare. Most cities are for all practical purposes one-newspaper towns. The competition now is between television networks. And between newspapers and television. Again, this competition can be either healthy or not. When it leads to saturation coverage of important issues and events such as those we've seen over the past several weeks — the *Challenger* tragedy, the Philippine upheaval — the competition is generally beneficial. But when it leads newspapers to try to imitate the immediacy, brevity, and superficiality of television, competition is of questionable value, for that shortsighted imitation robs the public of the most important service of newspapers and the print media, the ability to expand upon the basic facts with background information and with interpretation.

Make no mistake, interpretation is a necessary element of modern journalism, one especially needed for fair coverage of Indian concerns. Back in the terrible days of McCarthyism, it is now generally acknowledged, it was the lack of interpretation that allowed the Wisconsin senator to get away with unsubstantiated charges, intimidation and repression. Toeing the line of objectivity, reporters passed along what McCarthy said without comment, without context. The news became what he said, not his lack of substantiation or his flamboyant and paranoiac style. The result was some ten years in which writers and artists, journalists like William Shirer among them, were slandered and blacklisted. Moreover, the sheer weight of news today, its multiplicity and complexity, calls for some sorting out, some setting in perspective. Surely Indian concerns with broken treaties, attempts to regain or preserve land rights, require background exposition. Yet I have sat in on sessions with the Sioux Falls Area Press Association in which knowledgeable spokesmen have gone into background information in greater detail than was ever made readily available to the public at large. And I have been impressed not only with the volume of information made available in such sessions but also with how few of the reporters present were taking notes or making tapes and with how little of that information was ultimately passed along to the public. Even though the reporters indignantly insist that the proceedings be on the record, very little gets on the air or into print. The radio and television reporters have an excuse they are quick to invoke — the lack of time. But if issues are really important, shouldn't time and space be made available?

Another insidious effect of the emphasis upon timeliness or immediacy, the effect that most hinders the communication of Indian concerns, is that it promotes public expectation of novelty and reduces the public patience for broader exposition. This may be called the pop-journalism effect, a natural offshoot of the pop-music aesthetic. If novelty is seen as the essential ingredient of good journalism and anything over a half-day old is "ancient history," even the biggest news stories of our time can wear out their welcome. If you're old enough, you may remember how often you heard complaints about coverage of the Vietnam War or about Watergate. The essential complaint was that there was too much of it, that it was repetitious, "the same thing every night." I am convinced that these complaints were motivated not only by political partisanship but also by a general expectation of the public for novelty in the news. Indeed, the cave-in of public opinion and the resulting cave-in of official stances in these issues may very well have been the result more of public weariness with the reiteration of the stories than with any demonstrations of protest or with incisive investigative reporting.

Most of the concerns and issues affecting Indians are not perceived as being very new. The bungling of government bureaucracy, the poverty, housing, health problems, the problems with alcohol and drugs, the tribal politics, the continuing raids of Indian-owned land by individuals and corporations, the bigotry encountered among whites, the difficulties of cultural adaptation, the struggles with European ideas of justice—these issues are years, decades, scores of years old. Nobody denies that they are important, but it seems hard for many journalists to justify reporting on these issues without that essential element of novelty. When something new and therefore newsworthy does happen—a Wounded Knee takover, a Yellow-Thunder camp, an accusation about the governor's relationship with Indians—then the national press rushes in to cover it without restraint and sometimes without very good judgment. When the novelty wears off, the national press takes the next flight out and leaves the Indian pretty much where he was before. Such ephemeral events certainly call the attention of the press and of the public to the concerns of the Indian, but what is needed is for attention to remain on those concerns long enough for something to get done about them. And there is a need as well for the media to see that news about Indians is not all about problems, plights, difficulties, negatives. Again Tim Giago has led the way in showing that there are plenty of positive stories on the reservations: stories of Indians dealing with their concerns with great spirit and optimism and stories about the good, wholesome, everyday things that constitute life on the reservation.

By far the greatest of the idols of the theater is the principle of prominence. This touchstone for newsworthiness emphasizes celebrity, personalities, the names that make news. Again, this principle is far from being new, but the universal application of it in the news of our time seems somewhat unusual. The strangest thing is that it touches not only the news-makers but also the news-reporters. Names make news and names tell us the news. The model for the celebrity-as-reporter was Sir Henry Morton Stanley, who together with David Livingstone made up the Gallagher-Sheean act of African exploration. As a stunt to sell newspapers, the *New York Herald* sent Stanley to find Livingstone in Africa. Never mind that Livingstone wasn't really lost. The reporter finally caught up with Livingstone in the African interior and uttered the words that have become a catchphrase thanks to his own reporting of them and subsequent repetition in popular lore and motion pictures: "Doctor Livingstone, I presume?" Nobody remembers what Livingstone said. He died after another year. It was Stanley who reaped the harvest of notoriety. What a career: born in Wales, abandoned, adopted by an American, serving on both sides in the Civil War—first in the Confederate Army and later in the Union Navy—then as a reporter, then as explorer, then as a naturalized British subject, knighted, serving in parliament until 1900. Think what he might have done in the television age.

Perhaps the ultimate celebrity news-maker in the nineteenth century was George Armstrong Custer. You may question his good judgment, his morality, and his ambition, but you cannot question his talents as a publicity hound. In *Prelude to Glory* Gary D. Olson and Herbert Krause documented Custer's Black Hills Expedition, which took place just a couple years after Stanley's expedition to Africa. The expedition was an invasion of Indian territory especially sacred to the Sioux and was in violation of the Fort Laramie treaty guaranteeing the area to tribal custody. In addition to the soldiers in the party, there were guides, scouts, geologists, a photographer, and reporters from the *New York Tribune,* the *Chicago Inter-Ocean,* the *St. Paul Press,* the *St. Paul Pioneer,* and the *Bismarck Tribune* (Krause and Olson). The geologists were there to discover gold in the Hills, which they did. The reporters were there to sing Custer's praises and to send word back of the gold, good land and water, and other riches that the Black Hills held. Which they did. It was the beginning of the end of Indian ownership of the Hills. It was the beginning of the self-promotion that might have propelled Custer into politics, perhaps even into the presidency, if it had not been for his slight miscalculation at the Little Big Horn.

Given that history of journalism as theater, and given the additional impetus of television, which serves as a dream machine as well as an answer box, it is no wonder that the modern press seems always on the lookout for the ultimate celebrity, the ultimate personification, the ultimate spokesman. In Dr. Martin Luther King the media found just what they wanted, to the great benefit of the black civil rights movement and the enrichment of all Americans. But prophet-heroes like King are rare. In covering Indian concerns the press seeks in vain for the one man who speaks for the Indian. That is not to say that there have been no leaders. In fact, Vine Deloria, Jr., writes, "The Sioux problem is excessive leadership" (*Custer Died for Your Sins* 29). In the place of the single spokesman there is a polyphony of voices, a multitude of points of view. There is a strong pan-Indian spirit, binding the tribes across the nation — since the tribes have only recently discovered that they have much more in common with each other than with Anglo-European culture. But each tribe retains its own identity and collective personality, its own interests, certain problems and concerns that are unique. And within each tribe there is a complicated pattern of alliances and enmities. It is apparent to anyone looking on that it would be much better if each tribe could speak with one voice, better yet if all Native Americans could achieve the leverage that comes from unanimity. To the degree the black civil rights activists were drawn together behind the leadership of King, they were unstoppable. It seems apparent, as well, that it is in the interest of the enemies of Native Americans to use a devisive strategy, to set one Indian against another. But that does not mean that the press can recklessly identify anyone it likes to serve the messianic role for Indians. That role must be taken by someone the Indians like. Perhaps such a role was once possible for Russell Means or for Dennis Banks or for Clyde Bellecourt or some other emerging leader of the American Indian Movement. But for all practical purposes AIM is dismantled. Whether its failing health was the result of FBI subversion and government trickery and oppression, as Peter Matthiessen would have it, or whether it is naturally and inevitably moribund, due to flawed structure and lack of popular support, it seems done for. Yet out of habit the press, the national press at least, goes to former AIM leaders for statements and comments on any and every issue of interest to Indians. In a panel discussion at this conference a couple days ago, a television anchor said that when AIM comes up with something new, it gets reported. Perhaps the press just doesn't know anywhere else to go. Or perhaps it is too lazy or hasn't the time to listen to the multitude of voices and to try to forge some consensus from them.

The Native American scene today is indeed a confusing one. There are many guidebooks and many willing scouts, too many, it sometimes seems. And the maps don't always correspond to the territory. A selection must be made among guides, perhaps a new map drawn, a way picked out from the many criss-crossed paths. If the Indians won't "get their act together," or if they can't, if the major motion pictures and rock concerts do not come about to dramatize Indian concerns, and if the media sit waiting eagerly for some spokesman to arise, for something to happen that can get the message across in two minutes on the evening news — in other words, if things proceed as they have proceeded for the past decade or so — then there seems little hope for progress in the reporting on Indian affairs.

To conclude, a reminder that from some points of view the European culture is the "other," and that the idols I have spoken of affect all men, not just non-Indians. In the writing of George Catlin, the famous painter and chronicler of early Indian life on the plains, is a fascinating passage. Catlin is speaking to a Sioux chief in the 1830s, being a good reporter, taking notes, when suddenly the chief turns the tables on him and starts to ask about reports that have come back to the Indians concerning white customs:

> He also told me he had often heard that white people hung their criminals by the neck, and choked them to death like dogs, and those their own people; to which I answered, "yes." He then told me he had learned that they shut each other up in prisons, where they keep them a great part of their lives because they can't pay money! I replied in the affirmative to this, which occasioned great surprise and excessive laughter, even amongst the women. . . . He said . . . that he had been along the Frontier, and a good deal amongst the white people, and he had seen them whip their little children — a thing that is very cruel — he had heard also, from several white medicine-men, that the Great Spirit of the white people

was the child of a white woman, and that he was at last put to death by the white people! This seemed to be a thing that he had not been able to comprehend. . . . He put me a chapter of other questions as to the trespasses of the white people on their lands — their continual corruption of the morals of their women — and digging open the Indians' graves to get their bones, etc. To all of which I was compelled to reply in the affirmative, and quite glad to close my note-book and quietly to escape from the throng that had collected around me, and saying (though to myself and silently), that these and an hundred other vices belong to the civilized world, and are practiced upon (but certainly, in no instance, reciprocated by) the "cruel and relentless savage." (Catlin 2:756-57)

WORKS CITED

Arens, William. *The Man-Eating Myth.* New York: Oxford UP, 1979.

Catlin George. *Letters and Notes on the Manners, Customs, and Condition of the North American Indians.* 1941. 2 vols. Minneapolis: Ross and Haines, 1965.

Deloria, Vine, Jr. *We Talk, You Listen: New Tribes, New Turf.* New York: Dell, 1970.

— — —. *Custer Died for Your Sins.* New York: Macmillan, 1969.

Homer. *The Odyssey.* Trans. Robert Fitzgerald, *The Norton Anthology of World Masterpieces.* Ed. Maynard Mack, et al. New York: Norton, 1980, 226-300.

Krause, Herbert, and Gary D. Olson. *Prelude to Glory.* Sioux Falls, S.D.: Brevet, 1974.

Matthiessen, Peter. *In the Spirit of Crazy Horse.* New York: Viking, 1983.

Powers, William K. *Oglala Religion.* Lincoln: U of Nebraska P, 1975.

Women of the Circle

VIRGINIA DRIVING HAWK SNEVE

South Dakota author and teacher Virginia Driving Hawk Sneve presented this paper at the 1985 Berdahl-Rölvaag Lecture Series.

The circle is nature's most perfect form. To the Dakota/Lakota and other Indian tribes, the circle is a sacred symbol of life — life of the earth and all of the creatures inhabiting the land and the waters. Individual parts within the circle connect with every other; and what happens to one, or what one part does, affects all within the circle.

A great deal is known of that circle, yet our knowledge is incomplete because a vital part has been ignored — the women of the circle. This paper attempts to provide a brief history of these women from prereservation times up through World War I.

I have had to rely on oral information received from my grandmothers and other elderly women and men whom I have informally interviewed over thirty some years. It was necessary to engage in an unscholarly approach of reverse research. I have gone to written sources only to substantiate what I had already known of the women who were the center of the circle.

We know of the White Buffalo Calf Woman whose story was told by an Indian male and recorded by a white man. This familiar written version stresses that which is of importance to men.

Hear, now, the story as told by the women:

They say that somewhere over by the Pipestone Quarries, the people gathered to pray to Wakantanka. Two young men

were sent out to hunt. They walked along—they didn't have horses yet—until there was a bright light, or something, in front of them so that they had to stop.

Their eyes got used to the bright light; they saw a beautiful girl all dressed in white.

"I am from the Buffalo People," she said. "They sent me to talk to your people. I want you to go tell them that I will come to see them."

She was so pretty that one of the young men didn't listen well to what she was saying.

"Tell your people to have a council tipi ready for me," she told them. She told them how to set it up.

The young man who thought she was so pretty was not listening because he had bad thoughts about her. He tried to grab her.

"Don't!" the other young man yelled, but too late.

There was a crash of thunder, and a big cloud came over the bad man and the pretty girl. When it cleared away, the bad man was only a skeleton on the ground. Ever after the White Buffalo Calf Woman protects girls from bad men (Hassrick 20).

The other young man was afraid, but the woman told him that because he did not have bad thoughts, he would be all right. So he went back to his village and told the people all that had happened and what the woman told them to do.

The people were all excited. They got everything ready.

Then she came from the east with the sunrise, all dressed in white and so beautiful. In her hands she carried a pipe. She walked to the tipi. Its door opened to the east (which is why they are always set up that way). She walked in and turned to the left (which is why that is the women's side). She sat down with her legs placed to her right side and tucked her feet in (which is why women sit that way). When she talked everyone understood her, but the women noticed that some of the words she used were different from the way the men spoke (which is why women have a special way to talk).

She told the people about Wakantanka. She said that she was the people's sister and that she had brought them a sacred pipe. The pipe was for peace and not for war.

131

She talked to the women. "My sisters," she called them, "you have hard things to do in your life. You have pain when you have babies and it's hard to raise children. But you are important, because without you there wouldn't be any people. So you will have babies for your husband. You will feed your man and children; you will make their clothes; you will make the tipis. You will be good wives."

Then she spoke to the girls who weren't married. "You will be pure until you get married. Then you will always be faithful to your husband."

Then she talked to the men. "My brothers," she called them. "You must have good thoughts about girls so that they will be pure when they get married. When you take wives, you will be kind to all of them" (because she said "wives" the men could have more than one). She told them to be good to the children and to all the old people (which is why there were no orphans and all the old people where taken care of and respected).

She stayed with the people about four days and taught them how to use the pipe for healing and in seven sacred ceremonies. She left, walking to the east. She turned into a white buffalo calf (which is why nobody kills a white buffalo calf).

The above is a retelling of the White Buffalo Calf Woman story as it might have been told by one of my grandmothers. It differs from the way a man would tell the story, barely noting facts important to the men, but stressing those aspects vital to the women.

The story is an example of the oral tradition through which all American tribes transmitted their history. Another method of recording history was the winter count, in which pictographic drawings depicted an important yearly event. The winter count was usually prepared and kept by men who were concerned with events affecting the male. I studied the interpretations of three winter counts and found women depicted briefly, giving us only a glimpse of the hardships of women's life in the waning nomadic years and in the early days of reservation settlement (see Appendix).

All three of the winter counts span 151 years, with significant events of tribal experience depicted. Only twenty-one of those years noted episodes relating to women; thus, it is safe to assume

that they were uncommon or unique occurrences. The brief glimpse we get of women's lives during this era indicates that women were taken captive, but rarely were women killed (even an unfaithful wife), and suicide did occur. Women could return to their parents if their husbands were abusive, but it was unusual for the husband to pursue the woman and kill his inlaws. We know from oral sources that children were treasured by the tribe; thus, it was disastrous when women died in childbirth and more so when expectant mothers died. An old woman found dead in 1850-51 in a buffalo carcass was probably one who, because of illness or the rare time when an old woman had no one to care for her, was left to survive as best she could when the tribe moved. By 1838 and 1847, women marrying white men is documented.

All of the winter count data about women have been confirmed by oral sources, which were then frequently recorded by white men. A people without a written language, however, used the oral and pictographic method of keeping their history. These methods have not been given much credence by a society which relies on the written word.

When we come to written records, we again find scant information about women for the same reason that the winter counts ignored female events; that is, both were kept by men. Additionally, the white men who first encountered the Dakota/Lakota wrote from the point of view of their own culture in which — at that time — the activities of men were the only happenings worthy of note.

One of the earliest written records of encounters with Dakota women was in 1695 when LeSueur wrote that his party had found the Dakota wife of a Dakota chief held captive, a Macinaw. LeSueur bought her freedom and took her to Montreal where she was later reunited with her tribe (Robinson, *History of the Dakota* 42).

In 1700 LeSueur met a party of Dakota who told him of the Teton who lived on the prairies and related their customs, one of which was polygamy (Robinson, *History of the Dakota* 46). Generally, in these male written records Indian women were described as slaves and pawns in male economic transactions, or they were viewed idealistically as noble princesses. The work done by the women was viewed as second class as compared to the warrior hunter role (Weist 256-57). Women were reported as doing all of the essential chores while the male played at hunting and fishing. This judgment emerged from the European practice of idealizing women and from a period in European culture when hunting and fishing were recreational activities (Riley 31-32).

General Henry Sibley wrote that the man furnished his family with food and raw material for clothing, but the woman did everything else. He also noted, however, that the woman would be ashamed if her husband performed any of the female chores (*Reminiscences* 256).

Sibley's account verifies the oral information I received from my grandmothers and other sources. My grandmothers were wise, dignified, modest women who were also teachers, healers, and deeply religious, honest women. They were hard-working, proud of their husbands and of their virtuous faithfulness to them, and they considered children as a blessing. Their role was patterned after that of their prereservation mothers and grandmothers: to be a mate, companion, and homemaker to their husband and to bear and raise his children. Women were thought to have the power of life within them and, thus, the continuity of existence rested with them, as the White Buffalo Calf Woman had ordained.

Although none of my informants identified the practices of their female forebears as being part of the female value system, their statements agree with Royal Hassrick's identification of the Sioux women's virtues of bravery, generosity, truthfulness, and childbearing, with the ultimate achievement being motherhood (39, 41).

My oral sources used *women* and *motherhood* as nearly synonymous terms. Children, precious reason for a woman's existence, were considered to be the mother's property as were the contents of the lodge. Therefore, any activity which required too much time away from the lodge and/or the children was avoided. After menopause, however, a woman could seek visions (and a few did) and become a medicine woman, whose cessation of the menstrual cycle endowed her with powerful healing gifts (Weist 259).

The prereservation woman did indeed perform much hard physical labor, but it kept her lean and healthy and was not thought of as drudgery. The practice of polygamy lessened an individual wife's tasks. Men frequently married sisters, but the term *sister-wife,* by which wives addressed each other, did not mean that all of a man's wives were siblings. The more wives a man had, the more skins could be tanned for the comfort of the lodge. Women of one family worked together, but also helped other families in moving camp—dismantling and setting up the tipis—in midwifery, and in the technical and artistic knowledge of tanning and constructing lodge covers, clothing, quilling, and bead work (Weist 257). Formal societies were formed to share skills, to instruct, and to chaperone young girls. Grandmothers and mothers kept a strict eye on the girls—to keep them pure as the White Buffalo Calf Woman had directed.

It was an economic advantage for a man to have several wives, but the more women in his lodge the more he was controlled by them. When women of several lodges combined their forces, they had power over the men, both physically and psychologically, even though they may not have had a direct voice in the tribe's decision-making process (Weist 261).

With the advent of the fur trade came change and the deterioration of the female's status as husbands began bartering their wives' tanned skins for guns and whiskey. The traders dealt only with the Indian men, unaware that after they brought home the raw product, they no longer had control of the finished product (Weist 259). But even if the traders had known, they would not have considered dealing with the women, as women rarely engaged in commerce in the white world. Later, the Indian Service also dealt exclusively with the men.

The Dakota in Minnesota were the first to have frequent contact with white fur traders from the Canadian fur companies. A French Canadian, according to Doane Robinson, "considered it his first privilege to obtain an Indian wife," and the children of these mixed marriages were called *bois brules* (burnt woods) which had reference to their color (*History of the Dakota* 49).

The English and Scots from Canada also cohabited with Dakota women. In my own oral genealogy, it has been told that Hazzodowin, sister to the Santee chief Red Wing, "married" James Fraser but that he left her and their little boy to return to Canada. Research has authenticated that James Fraser, son of Scots-Catholic immigrants and brother of Simon, who discovered the Fraser River, in British Columbia, accompanied Zebulon Pike part way up the Mississippi in the fall of 1805 and wintered with Red Wing's band (Sibley, *Iron Face* xviii).

Oral and written history also notes that one of Red Wing's daughters married a Scots trader whose daughter became the mother of Charles Crawford and Gabriel Renville (Robinson, *History of the Dakota* 127).

In 1812 Major Robert Dickson, a British officer and trader and the western agent and superintendent of the Indian Department, married a Dakota woman. Unnamed in written history, she was the sister of Red Thunder, a Yanktonnais chief. This marriage is reputed to have established a special tie to the Mississippi Dakota tribes which influenced their participation as English allies in the War of 1812 (*South Dakota Historical Collections* 33:39).

The second most widely known Indian woman, after Pocahantas, is Sacajawea, without whom Lewis and Clark might not have reached the Pacific. These explorers kept a journal of their travels, faithfully noting the flora, fauna, and place names given to various waters and lands. In these official records, they also noted the various Indians they encountered, but it is only through oral history that we know that Meriwether Lewis fathered at least one son while sojourning among the tribes.[1] Oral history also tells us that Clark had "married" a Nez Perce woman, who refused to accompany him east.

Charbonneau, Dorion, and Drouillard served as guides for the Lewis and Clark expedition, having been long-established traders in the area. Their Indian wives had given the men an economic advantage in the fur trade because of the availability of ready pelts from the women's tribes. The women cared for their white husbands as they would have an Indian husband, and their female relatives helped care for his furs. The trader

136

himself gained the protection of his wife's tribe since through marriage he became a relative. The women and their parents considered it an honor for the girl to be a white man's wife, as he gave them horses, trinkets, iron kettles, guns, and whiskey. There were hundreds of such arrangements made with women of the Sioux tribes. Some of these traders, like my own great-grandfather, Basil (Baptiste) Clement (Claymore), roamed, trapped, traded, and cohabited all over the territories—from Canada to St. Louis, from the Mississippi to the Rockies. (*North Dakota Historical Collections* 1:341).

South Dakota historian Doane Robinson frequently notes that men who worked for the fur companies had Indian wives: Joseph Garreau, Joseph La Framboise, David LaChapelle, LaRoche, Kenneth McKenzie, Charles Primeau, Joseph Renville, and Zephyr Recontre. (*History of the Dakota*). Unfortunately, Robinson does not tell us the names of the Indian wives.

George Kingsbury's history of Dakota Territory, recording the deeds of the traders, notes that the traders had Sioux wives, but, again, omitted their names. George Catlin, however, describes the Sioux wife of William Laidlaw as "fine looking, modest and dignified . . . the kind and affectionate mother of his [Laidlaw's] little flock of pretty and interesting children" (qtd. in Kingsbury 1:45).

Other traders who may or may not be noted in history books are Amiotte, Antoine, Bordeaux, Desera, Dewitt, Dubray, Dupris, Gordon, Kimmel, LaPlante, LaPionte, Rosseau, Roubaix, Roubideaux, Rouse, St. Pierre, Traversie, and Verendrye. It is through the oral histories of their descendants that we know these men had Sioux wives—and from the enrollment of their descendants as members of South Dakota tribes.

Women who married French men, whether from Canada or from the American fur companies of New Orleans or St. Louis, found little change had to be made in their lives, for the French men adopted Sioux customs and language. Indeed, they were often called "French Indians." Women who married Anglo-Saxon men became bilingual and had to adapt to their husbands' lifestyles. These men were called "Squaw Men," which, along with "French Indian," was a derogatory label given by white society, which generally thought of Indian women as being fiendish, immoral snares who entrapped civilized men.

At first, an Indian woman thought it at honor to cohabit with a white man, but she soon found that her life had become a life of drudgery. Rarely was there a "sister-wife" to share her household and conjugal duties; she gave birth more frequently and over a longer period of time and, as a result, suffered more in childbirth. Her status was lower and she was often physically abused. In the early fur trade years, such a woman returned to her family and was accepted, as were her children; later, she became an outcast as her former alliance was considered shameful. The most difficult aspect for these women to accept was that all of the goods in the house were the property of the man; therefore, she lost control of her home and of her children.

After the decline of the fur trade, many of the traders stayed with their Indian wives and children, but many more returned to civilization, either abandoning wives and children or leaving the wife and taking the children to be raised as whites. Oral sources tell of such women hanging themselves in despair or following the children to live in poverty on the outskirts of the white man's city, experiencing the final, unbearable shame of children disowning their Indian mother.

At other times, as adults, the children returned to their mother's tribes to live as Indians. Such was the situation of Charles Picotte, whose father had educated him in St. Louis but who had left two daughters with their mother (Robinson, *History of the Dakota* 249). The mother, Eagle Woman, later married Major Charles E. Galpin; she was one of the lucky ones who found another husband after being abandoned by the first (Sansom-Flood and Bernie 7).

By now, all tribes had become distrustful of the whites, and the cast-aside wives were thought unworthy to be mates of Indian males. The abandoned children, neither white nor Indian, were in limbo. Their mothers had instilled in them pride in having a white man for a father, but the mixed-blood offspring often had an overbearing pride in their white blood, which offended the full-bloods (O'Meara 251). The mixed-blood daughter, most often abandoned with the mother, fared better than her brothers.

She was an acceptable wife to Indian men, to mixed-blood males, and to white men who came to settle permanently in Dakota.

The large numbers of "French Indians" who settled in Dakota with their wives were counted in the 1859 census. The population of Dakota Territory seemed to have exploded by 1870 because the large numbers of mixed-blood offspring could be counted and they were more numerous than that of whites (Kingsbury 1:82-84). These French were joined by later-arriving white men who came to Dakota for commerce or with the military and married Indian women.

True Woman, a full-blood Oglala, was given the name Julia at her baptism and marriage to Charles P. Jordan. Jordan, a cousin of George A. Custer, was a licensed Indian trader on the Rosebud (Hamilton and Hamilton 127). Julia was photographed by John A. Anderson and is one of the few full-blood women about whom a great deal is known. She was awarded the first allotment on the Rosebud, which she selected and upon which Jordan built a large house and operated a ranch (Hamilton and Hamilton 31).

As Dakota opened up to homesteaders, white ranchers and farmers came, and some of them married Indian women. Scotty Philip's wife, Sarah, was one of these Indian women, and she influenced him to raise buffalo, which were almost extinct by that time (Lee 442).

Military men, upon mustering out, frequently elected to stay in Dakota, and a number of them married Indian women. For example, trooper Enoch Raymond and his friend Joseph Ross, a civilian Army freighter, married sisters of the Oglala Fire Thunder band. The women took allotments along the Keyapaha River on which their husbands operated ranches.

The military presence among the tribes resulted in a number of similar alliances, but, again, few of the Indian wives' names are found in written history. Oral history can be substantiated by church records *if* the couple was married by clergy or the woman and/or her children were baptized.

Many Indian women were not so respected as to be wed by soldiers. As Indian men became addicted to alcohol, fathers, brothers, and husbands traded their daughters, sisters, and wives for drink. Prostitution in the Sioux tribes did not exist until alcohol. In a warrior society, where women outnumbered men, there was no need. Polygamy also made prostitution unnecessary.

Oral stories from several sources relate many incidents of women being traded for liquor to soldiers. Fort Laramie is best known as the site of treaty negotiations, but it is infamous for the alcohol-related abuse of women. Total demoralization of the tribe occurred as mothers in their drunkenness gave alcohol to their children (Nadeau 36-39).

To celebrate a victory over a tribe, troopers often rounded up the prettiest girls to be passed among the officers, leaving the enlisted men with less attractive older women. One of my oral informants, who does not wish to be named, tells of her Cheyenne grandmother, the daughter of Black Kettle, whom Custer killed in the raid at the Washita. She was one of several pretty married and unmarried girls taken by the officers after the battle. Because of her status as the chief's daughter, she went to Custer. When Custer moved on, she found herself pregnant and unacceptable as a wife to any man of her tribe. She bore a son and lived in destitution until an Oglala man pitied her, took her to Pine Ridge, gave her son his name, and raised him as his own.

But what of the Indian women who did not cohabit with whites but settled on the reservations? We know more of the pioneer white women who settled in Dakota; from them we can learn about their Indian counterparts. Grace Fairchild, who came to Dakota in 1898, wrote, "I always felt I had a lot in common with the Indian mothers even if we lived on different sides of the fence" (Wyman 39). And when we compare the lives of the women of the two races, we find that they did have much in common. Both spent most of their time at work and play with children and other women; even at mixed gatherings men and women congregated separately.

To document my oral dates of those first Indian women on the reservation, I have found the best source to be Elaine Goodale Eastman's memoirs. Elaine Goodale came to the Lower Brulé Episcopal Mission in 1886, where she worked with Indian women and taught their children. During the five years she lived in Dakota, she recorded her experiences in articles for eastern publications. On her arrival at Lower Brulé, Goodale wrote, "We found . . . two distinct worlds existing side by side, now in dramatic opposition, now intimately mixed. There were already a few Dakotas at home in the white man's world. . . . There were also a good many of both races who belonged as much to one as to the other" (qtd. in Graber 33).

Plural marriages among the elderly were still condoned, but if a man became Christian he could have only one wife, causing a great deal of distress for the abandoned wife and her children.

Rarely did a prereservation woman remain unmarried; as noted earlier, it was her lot to be wife and mother. If widowed, her husband's brother, brother-friend, or close male relative would take the woman and her children as part of his family. But in those early reservation years, after plural marriages were outlawed, there were not enough men to go around. Unwed women became an oddity and objects of pity.

The male warrior-hunter was without purpose on the reservation, and he, too, became a pitiful thing. His former role totally destroyed, he frequently turned to alcohol to ease his distress. The women were the steadying center of the family. Many also became the bread winners by selling their quill, bead, and other craft work.

Women also became the spiritual center of the family. They were converted to Christianity with their husbands, but it was easier for them to live their new religion as they had done in the old way. Their role as wife and mother was essentially unchanged from prereservation life when religion was an integral element. It permeated every thought and act, and so did Christianity. White women missionaries and teachers, like Elaine Goodale, trained Indian women to use the sewing machine and cook new foods on stoves, while at the same time they taught the Gospel.

At each Episcopal mission station, Bishop Hare reported, little bands of Indian women, aided by the white women, formed guilds. A formal society was natural to the women, but now their purpose differed. They saved their pennies or did quill and beadwork to make money to build a chapel. They not only contributed to the expenses of their own congregation, but also to the native clergy fund, missions in Japan, orphanages in China, the church schools in Dakota, and innumerable other enterprises (Sneve 87).

In 1893 Cora Saxton, one of the first white women on the Pine Ridge, helped give Christian names from the Bible to Indian women converts (who now bore their husband's names) along with yards of bright calico (*South Dakota History Collections* 33:65). The women learned to sew the calico and fashioned the long-sleeved, ankle-length, shapeless gowns now considered the dress of the traditional Indian woman.

Change came slowly. Customs of child rearing, courtship, marriage, and homemaking remained almost the same up to the time of World War I—despite boarding schools. The isolation of the people on the reservation kept the traditions and customs alive, and the women held the families together.

Elaine Goodale wrote of Indian women's work as being many tasks, but always cheerfully done. She never saw Indian women treated as slaves or beasts, but as equals and companions to men (Graber 104). This indicates that those Indians who had little contact with the whites retained the women's status and the importance of their role as wife and mother. Futhermore, they still thought virginity until marriage and faithfulness afterwards were important. Goodale found young girls strictly chaperoned by their grandmothers. "No virtuous girl," she wrote, "or young married woman . . . " dared "to meet men openly" and to look them in the eye, nor talk with them (qtd. in Graber 49). If she did, her reputation was damaged and her family shamed:

> Dear, lovable, intensely feminine Sioux women of days gone by! How affectionately I recall their devotion to their families . . . . When I first went to live among them, old customs were beginning to lose validity, but had by no means been forgotten. It was a period of changing manners and conflicting codes. (qtd. in Graber 34, 49)

By now, the women had become dependent on the men for subsistence because of the government's commodity distribution dealings with male heads of family; however, they still had autonomy at home. As in the past, when all in the lodge was hers, so now all in the log cabin was hers in that she cared for it and saw to the distribution of the commodity foods. Even as late as the 1930s, reservation women were performing traditional domestic chores and providing stability in a disorganized reservation society (Mirsky 418-22). This was found to be true of mixed-blood as well as full-blood women.

To the historic virtues of the Sioux women, resilience and adaptability should be added, for they were tough enough to survive and yet could change within their traditional roles. By the mid-forties, an Indian woman's position in the family had risen to be more important than that of the men (MacGregor 118).

The White Buffalo Calf Woman said that without the women there would be no people. The Dakota/Lakota women's strength and spirituality kept the people alive during that difficult transition period of early contact with the whites and reservation settlement. They truly became the center of the circle.

APPENDIX

WINTER COUNTS

1775-1855[2]	Big Missouri 1796-1926[3]
1784-85	A captive Omaha woman tried to escape, but was killed.	
1792-93	Many women died in childbirth.	
1797-98	An Arikara woman was killed while gathering turnips. A captured enemy woman claimed to be a spirit.	

1798-99	Many women died in child-birth.	A very cold winter caused the death of many expectant women.
1804-05	A woman who was un-faithful to her husband was killed by a man named Ponka.	
1805-06		A delegation of Indians and their wives went to Washington.
1828-29		A young woman, abused by her husband, fled to her father, Walking Crow. Her husband pursued her, at-tacked the father, then returned to his own tipi. Walking Crow followed the husband and shot and killed him.
1834-35		A Cheyenne, married to a Sioux girl during peace be-tween the tribes, deserted her when war began. After the war was over, he re-turned, but the Sioux killed him.
1838-39	Iron Horn, father of Mrs. Frederick Dupree, built a dirt lodge on the Moreau River.	A man from Broken Bow's camp stole the wife of a man from another camp. This caused such bad feel-ings that the Broken Bow man was killed.
1847-48	Big Thunder's wife bore twins.	Tall Joe, a white man, and his Sioux wife lost a grown son to drowning.

Big Missouri 1796-1926[4]   **1800-1879**

| 1850-51 | | An old woman was found dead in the carcass of a buffalo. |

1857-58   A Crow woman was killed
                                                   by the Dakotas.

1883-84   Dog Shield died. His griev-
           ing wife hanged herself and
           they were buried together.

1887-88   Two women had bloated
           stomachs from an unknown
           ailment. The agency doctor
           tapped their stomachs, but
           they died.

1891-92   Two head of cattle issued
           to every man, woman, and
           child.

1893-94   The first per capita payment
           of $30.00 to every man,
           woman, and child.

1902-03   A man killed a woman in
           order to elope with her
           daughter.

1904-05   Leader Charger's wife gave
           birth to quadruplets.

1915-16   A cruel man killed his in-
           laws because they refused to
           return their daughter to
           him.

1918-19   Two girls deserted St. Fran-
           cis School on a very cold
           day. One froze to death; the
           other had to have her frozen
           feet amputated.

NOTES

[1]General editor's note: The parish registers for St. Philip the Deacon, White Swan, South Dakota (1:10-11; 2:48-49), located in the Archives of the Episcopal Diocese of South Dakota, the Center for Western Studies, Augustana College, record the baptism of Joseph DeSomet Lewis, sixty-eight years of age, on 18 June 1872. Both entries give Lewis' place of birth as Yankton Agency and his parents' names as "Capt. Meriwether Lewis (of Lewis & Clarke's [sic] Exp.) [and] Winona."

[2]"Sioux Calendar," *Doane Robinson's Encyclopedia of South Dakota,* 1925.

[3]*Buechel Memorial Lakota Museum* (St. Francis, S.D.: St. Francis Indian Mission, 1973).

[4]Joseph H. Cash, *The Sioux People* (Phoenix: Indian Tribal Series, 1971), 104.

WORKS CITED

Cash, Joseph H. *The Sioux People.* Phoenix: Indian Tribal Series, 1971.

Graber, Kay, ed. *Sister to the Sioux: The Memoirs of Elaine Goodale Eastman, 1885-91.* Lincoln and London: U of Nebraska P, 1978.

Hamilton, Henry W., and Jean Tyree Hamilton. *The Sioux of the Rosebud: A History in Pictures.* Norman: U of Oklahoma P, 1971.

Hassrick, Royal B. *The Sioux: Life and Customs of a Warrior Society.* Norman: U of Oklahoma P, 1964.

Kingsbury, George W. *History of Dakota Territory.* 2 vols. Chicago: Clarke, 1915.

Lee, Shebby. "Scotty Philip—The Man Who Saved the Buffalo." *14th Dakota History Conference Papers.* Comp. H. W. Blakely. Madison, S.D.: Dakota State College, 1983, 439-51.

MacGregor, Gordon. *Warriors Without Weapons: A Study of the Society and Personality Development of the Pine Ridge Sioux.* Chicago: U of Chicago P, 1946.

Mirsky, Jeannette. "The Dakota." *Cooperation and Competition Among Primitive Peoples.* Ed. Margaret Mead. Boston: Beacon, 1961, 382-427.

Nadeau, Remi. *Fort Laramie and the Sioux Indians.* Englewood Cliffs, N.J.: Prentice-Hall, 1967.

North Dakota Historical Collections. Vol. 1. Bismarck: State Historical Society of North Dakota, 1906.

O'Meara, Walter. *Daughters of the Country: The Women of the Fur Traders and Mountain Men.* New York: Harcourt, Brace & World, 1968.

Riley, Glenda. *Women and Indians on the Frontier, 1825-1915.* 1938. Albuquerque: U of New Mexico P, 1984.

Robinson, Doane. *A History of the Dakota or Sioux Indians.* 1904. Minneapolis: Ross and Haines, 1956.

— — —. *History of South Dakota.* Vol. 1. Chicago and New York: American Historical Society, 1930.

Sansom-Flood, Renée and Shirley A. Bernie. *Remember Your Relatives: Yankton Sioux Images, 1851-1904.* Marty, S.D.: Marty Indian School, 1985.

Sibley, H. H. "Reminiscences of the Early Days of Minnesota." *Minnesota Historical Collections.* Vol. 3. Saint Paul: Minnesota Historical Society, 1880, 242-82.

Sibley, Henry Hastings. *Iron Face: The Adventures of Jack Frazer, Frontier Warrior, Scout, and Hunter.* Ed. Theodore C. Blegen and Sarah A. Davidson. Chicago: Caxton Club, 1950.

"Sioux Calendar." *Doane Robinson's Encyclopedia of South Dakota.* 1925.

Sneve, Virginia Driving Hawk. *That They May Have Life: The Episcopal Church in South Dakota, 1859-1976.* New York: Seabury, 1977.

South Dakota History Collections. Vol. 33. Pierre: South Dakota Historical Society, 1966.

Weist, Katherine M. "Plains Indian Women: An Assessment." *Anthropology on the Great Plains.* Ed. W. Raymond Wood and Margot Liberty. Lincoln and London: U of Nebraska P, 1980, 255-71.

Wyman, Walker D. *Frontier Woman: The Life of a Woman Homesteader on the Dakota Frontier.* River Falls: U of Wisconsin-River Falls P, 1972.

Community and Tradition in Native American Society

DONNA J. HESS

A professor of rural sociology at South Dakota State University, Donna J. Hess presented this paper at the 1984 Berdahl-Rölvaag Lecture Series.

The focus of this presentation is on Native American values and Native American communities in the context of social and cultural change. More specifically, given the diversity of Native American cultural traditions and the concern of the Nordland Fest with "Siouxland" traditions, this presentation will deal primarily with the Dakota Indian (and particularly the Teton) complex of values and communities.

In considering values and communities in the context of social and cultural change, a basic premise will be developed in this presentation: that values are standards of desirability that people develop in relation to the experiences that they have in the world around them. If this is so, then it is proposed that traditional values persist over time to the extent that there is continuity in experiences with the world; and values change over time as experience with the world changes. As people's experiences vary, so too will their values vary. In sum, it is proposed here that values, like cultures more generally, represent people's adaptive responses to their world.

There is convincing support for this line of argument in the social science literature on values. For example, Milton Rokeach argues that there is a basic core of human values and that value systems vary in terms of the priorities that people assign to values. Priorities represent both people's assessments of the intrinsic worth of particular values and their perceptions of how problematic it is to realize particular values. The value of cleanliness provides a good illustration of this point. Rokeach found that black Americans ranked cleanliness third (in a set of eighteen values) while white Americans ranked cleanliness tenth (in the same set of eighteen values). Further, he observed that low income people ranked cleanliness second while higher income people ranked it seventeenth. In fact, he observed a consistent inverse linear relationship between the priority accorded cleanliness and people's income status. Rokeach suggested that these differences in priority were primarily due to cleanliness being more problematic for blacks (who are often lower in income) than for whites (who are more often higher in income and thus more able to take cleanliness for granted).

Perhaps an even better demonstration of the relationship between experiences in the world and values is found in Melvin Kohn's work. Kohn observes that there is a rather consistent relationship between social class and parental values (that is, parents' standards of desirability for their children). Middle-class parents, he found, gave higher priority to self-direction — thinking for oneself, making one's own decisions, developing internalized rules for behavior. Working-class parents, on the other hand, he found, gave higher priority to obedience and conformity — looking to authorities for direction, following rules, and paying close attention to the standards developed by others. Why are there these class differences in parental values? Kohn argued that they are largely due to differences in work experiences of middle- and working-class parents. Middle-class parents tend to be employed in positions which emphasize or require self-direction while working-class parents tend to be employed in positions which emphasize or require following directions, obeying rules, and conforming to the demands of others (foremen, superintendents, etc.).

What, you may ask, do these observations have to do with Native American values and communities? I contend that the same model or line of reasoning applies. That is, depending upon the community of experience of Native Americans, they will either hold to and express traditional Native American values or hold to and express less traditional Native American values. Understanding Native American values, and the diversity that presently exists among them and the changes that have occurred, requires understanding the communities of experience of Native Americans.

The traditional Native American (Teton Dakota) community of one hundred fifty or two hundred years ago (before extensive European-American influence) was best understood in terms of the family. In fact, Maynard and Twiss observed, "Between the family and the tribe stand the community. Formerly the family and the community were oftentimes synonymous" (129). The functional community in the traditional Dakota society was the extended family group—or *tiyospaye,* in Lakota. The term *tiyospaye* itself is derived from two root words: *ti* meaning "house" or "dwelling" and *ospaye* meaning "a company separated from the main body" (Grobsmith 20). Thus, the *tiyospaye,* or extended family, was a community of kinsmen who dwelled apart from other such groups in their band and who supported themselves through communal hunting. "This native community was organized for political purposes under the leadership of a 'headman' who exercised judgment and made decisions pertaining to hunting, food distribution, and location of the camp" (Grobsmith 21).

The band was, in fact, a relatively loose association of extended families who came together for larger communal hunts (usually in early fall when the hunting was good) and for ceremonial occasions (like the annual Sun Dance held in the summer). In this traditional society, there was no question of community membership or participation: " . . . membership was basically a matter of participation and kinship: those born into a band and participating in its life were its members, and those who might (rarely) leave and join (usually marry into) another band were members of that second band" (Wax 72). Thus, community identity was an identity based upon kinship, and community participation was the exercise of the rights and obligations associated with kinship.

The world of the Plains, inhabited by these kin-communities and bands, was a world of danger, uncertainty, and hardship. They followed a hunting and warring lifestyle. Warfare with other unrelated peoples (like the Crow, the Pawnee, the Shoshone, and the Arikara for the Dakotas) occupying the same general territory of the northern Plains was frequent. Livelihood, dependent upon roaming herds of buffalo and other game animals, was uncertain, and there were periods of famine as well as periods of plenty. There was a concept of territory among these people — with each band and each extended family within the band laying claim to use rights to particular territories and the resources of those territories. Defense and invasion of these territories were a common basis for warfare.

Traditional Dakota values were adaptive to these life circumstances. Four essential values were said to compose the "moral code" of Dakota life (MacGregor 106; Hassrick 32). "Bravery, fortitude, generosity, and wisdom — these were the virtues which all men were expected to seek. While it was understood that no man could achieve excellence in all of these qualities, it was believed that every man should endeavor to attain something of each" (Hassrick 32).

The value of bravery was clearly an important survival value in the world of the Plains peoples. It enabled the Dakota to face the many dangers of life on the Plains — dangers associated with hunting the buffalo as well as dangers associated with warfare. Hassrick reports a maxim of Dakota existence: "It is better to die on the battlefield than to live to be old" (32). He goes on to explain:

Of the four great values, bravery was foremost for both men and women. To be considered full of courage, to have a strong heart, was an honor of extreme importance and worth great effort. Acclaim was accorded only to those who had proven themselves. These were the daring men who deliberately risked their lives in war, who took chances in battle which could only be called dangerous,

151

who defended themselves against obvious odds. Just as a man might show deliberate courage in fighting the grizzly bear, the most ferocious and relentless of all animals, so might a woman display bravery in killing an enemy, in warding off an attacker, or in protecting her family against any harm. Bravery among women was equally as meritorious and deserving of recognition as it was among men. (32)

Bravery, however, was more than the show of courage. It also involved the display of wit and cunning. Thus, the counting of coup on an enemy—striking the enemy without killing him and getting away to tell the tale—was said to be the highest display of bravery (Bryde 27-28). Again, Hassrick relates:

> . . . the development of the concept of unflinching bravery was a practical preparation for Sioux adulthood, when the fine line between life and death was an ominous actuality. To be recognized as brave, an adult must exhibit fearlessness and the battlefield offered outstanding opportunities. Courting death became as important a part of warfare as victory, so much so that acts of valor were classified in a recognized system of war honors. Men who "struck" the enemy were said to have "counted coup," and whether or not the enemy was killed or wounded, the record was not jeopardized. The fact that a man was courageous enough to "touch" an opponent and risk death rather than shoot him from a safer distance showed the caliber of courage which the Sioux pattern prescribed. (33)

The value of fortitude was also related to the dangers, uncertainties, and hardships associated with the traditional world of the Plains. MacGregor explains:

> It was not only courage in battle but the enduring courage which enabled them to accept long hardships and to suffer pain and the self-inflicted tortures of their ceremonials.

152

This quality of fortitude has sustained the people through much adversity. (106-07)

One could not be certain, for example, that the hunt would be successful and that the family would have adequate food. Famine was always a possibility and did indeed occur. Similarly, one could not be certain that the outcome of a battle would be favorable; death or capture at the hands of an enemy was always a possibility. People adapted to these circumstances with a willingness to endure—with fortitude. As Hassrick points out, "Fortitude implied two things: the endurance of physical discomfort and pain, and the ability to show reserve during periods of emotional stress" (34). The importance of this value in the traditional life of the Dakota is noted by Hassrick:

The importance of the quality of fortitude was demonstrated again and again in the social conventions of the Sioux. Men on war missions or hunting expeditions were noted for this ability to suffer wounds unflinchingly, to experience long periods of hunger and exposure. Fortitude dictated the voluntary acceptance of physical pain during burial ceremonies, when the mourners were required to subject themselves to self-inflicted slashings on arms or legs, or to endure the agony of tiny skewers inserted beneath their skin, or to cut off the first joint of their little finger—all in order to show respect for the dead. (34)

Children, too, learned and displayed these prescribed rules of reserved behavior. Thus, Hassrick observes, "It was expected that young people should not speak their opinion before more mature minds. Rather, children were to sit quietly and absorb knowledge, for respect for elders marked the well-bred person" (35). To endure hardship and pain and to show reserve were the essence of the value of fortitude.

The third great value, generosity, was also responsive to the conditions of life experienced by the Dakota. Survival depended upon collective, cooperative efforts—in hunting, in warfare, in caring for the young, and in gathering plant foods and herbs. Again, Hassrick cites another precept of Dakota society in relation to this value: "A man must help others as much as possible, no matter who, by giving him horses, food or clothing" (36). In the context of this communal spirit, individual possessiveness would have been unthinkable and most inappropriate. "To accumulate property for its own sake was disgraceful. . . . The ownership of things was important only as a means to giving, and blessed was the man who had much to give" (36).

A sense of reciprocity was associated with the concept of generosity. Thus, while one was expected to share and give gifts, the recipient was also expected to make a return (even though a token) at some future time. This exchange was central to Dakota life:

> Young people brought food to their elders' tipis; hunters divided their kill with the aged and infirm; women made gifts for the orphaned and the widowed; sisters honored their brothers with presents of moccasins, or their nieces and nephews with elaborate cradles. (Hassrick 36-37)

MacGregor writes of the "give-away" as "a dramatic ceremony of distributing all of one's own belongings . . . [as] a means of honoring others and gaining social prestige. By making gifts in the name of a child or deceased member of the family, a relative showed his love or his grief. . . . Such a system functioned without permanently ruining the givers, for everyone gave and in turn received gifts at subsequent ceremonies" (107). Thus, generosity was the expression of cooperativeness and community under conditions requiring sharing and helpfulness.

The fourth and final value of the traditional Dakota moral code also grew out of the community of experience of the Dakotas. In their traditional communities, the people turned to their elders for advice and counsel. These older members of the community were recognized and respected for their insight and good judgment, which came from many years of experience and reflection upon that experience. MacGregor observes that "In the family the grandfathers were respected for their wisdom and were

154

expected to pass it on to their grandsons" (107). "Wisdom was also dependent upon power—insight received from the supernatural," according to Hassrick (39). One who possessed wisdom was able to advise others, to arbitrate disputes, to instill confidence in a war party, and to serve as mentor for the young. Great respect was accorded such individuals, for, as Hassrick observes the old Lakota to say, such individuals "seemed to have the power of helping and their word was as if from the Gods" (39).

In sum, the traditional value system of the Dakota peoples reflected their successful adaptation to their community of experience with life on the Plains. In a sense, one might even go so far as to say that their particular values were mandated for survival in that world.

In the mid-to-late nineteenth century, Native American communities on the Plains, including those of the Dakotas, underwent marked dislocations and changes. It was during this period that the reservations were created, and the diverse Dakota bands and extended family communities were required to settle on them. Restrictions were imposed on their former hunting and warring lifestyles. They were to take up a new lifestyle—agriculture. This new lifestyle was to be carried out in a way very different from their traditional ways, for the land to be reserved was to be individually allotted rather than held and used in common. MacGregor, in his study of reservation communities on the Pine Ridge Reservation of South Dakota, points out that there were attempts by *tiyospaye* members to settle on the reservation in proximity to one another:

> This pattern of the extended family living on adjoining lands was created in part by the allotment system, when a man, his wife, and children received adjoining allotments of land. As the children grew up and married, they built their homes on their own allotments, thereby retaining the family grouping and establishing a family neighborhood. (67)

Murray Wax, however, points out that this particular pattern did not always obtain. "When the reservations were coming into existence," Wax notes, "many persons associated themselves with war chiefs whose authority was sometimes reinforced by a tactical alliance with the Indian agent, who then proceeded to distribute rations through the mediation of the chief" (75). The outcome of these two patterns was the establishment of diverse kinds of communities on the reservations—some preserving the traditional *tiyospaye* communities, and others more heterogeneous and oriented to the political and economic systems of the dominant society. This, to a large extent, contributed to growing competition and rivalry among reservation communities, a situation often not understood by the government agents, according to Wax:

> While to an outsider the reservation might seem equivalent to a single society or "nation" composed of a single Indian people, speaking a common language and sharing many traits, to the inhabitants themselves there is no such unity, since they are first and foremost members of bands of kith and kin. In contrast the Indian agent and his associates have been charged with administering the reservation as a whole, so they have had to introduce reservation-wide institutions. Correspondingly, when the federal government stimulated development of tribal governments [in 1934], these were established on a reservation-wide or even multireservation basis. Traditional Indians have meanwhile continued to maintain their participation in, and allegiance to, their local band communities. (75)

Thus, " . . . Indian communities which were once culturally homogeneous and knit together into a tightly cooperative social fabric have been subject to intensive pressures from a highly diversified aggregate of missionaries, traders, soldiers, and governmental administrators" (Wax 73). Not only did the political community change from a homogeneous kin-based community to a heterogeneous community with no traditional basis for identification and cooperation, but many of the underpinnings of the traditional local community were also eroded with the establishment of the reservations. The practice of allotting reservation lands to individuals became official federal policy with the Dawes

Act of 1887, interpreted by many as a direct assault on the cooperative unit of the extended family. Similarly, reliance upon the wisdom of headmen and elders in decision making was to be replaced with dependence upon decision making by non-kin and government agents outside of the traditional community.

Over the years, other assaults have been made on the local community of the extended family and its ability to support and care for its own. For example, shortly after the Civil War, the concept of federal off-reservation boarding schools came to dominate federal policy in Indian education. Children were removed from their homes and communities not only for the duration of the school year but also for the summer months when they were placed in non-Indian homes to prevent their "return to the blanket." Similarly, William Byler cites social policy which has been hostile to cooperative kin relations in childcare, resulting in "the wholesale separation of Indian children from their families" (1). Then in the late 1940s and the late 1950s, the federal relocation program was instituted, further straining the extended family by urging what some have termed "the cream of the crop" to leave the reservation for often distant urban areas. While, in some cases, this only resulted in kin relations being extended over geographic distance, in other cases, it contributed to the demise of those relations. MacGregor summarizes these sociopolitical changes:

> Several factors, such as the geographic separation of families and the development of new extended family groups, have led to the disintegration of the original band groups. The individual and the individual family can, if they desire, support themselves on a farm or by wage work without the assistance of others and can find companionship and social life outside the community. . . . The band integration has also been weakened by the decline of Indian leadership and the passing of the functions of government to the Agency. . . . The loosening of Indian social and political organization and the absence of full recognition by the government of either the existing native communities or their traditional functions

and continuing potentialities for economic, social, and political organization and development are producing community disintegration. This disintegration and the development of individualism are resulting in insecurity for the group and the individual which are major problems of Dakota adjustment to reservation and white life. (68)

Contemporary Native American communities, then, are characterized by diversity, often dissension, and sometimes disorganization. Underscoring this characterization, Maynard and Twiss observe, "There is considerable variation in the degree of cohesiveness of the communities, but in general one can say that community organization has become diffuse and community pride has waned" (129). Value orientations, too, have become diverse — in adaptation to varying communities of experience.

Two distinct worlds of experience are encountered by Native American peoples today. There is the rural, reservation world — the world experienced by about 50% of the Native American population in the United States (and by about 74% in South Dakota). There is also the urban world — the world experienced by the remaining 50% of the Native American population in the United States (and by about 26% in South Dakota). It is important to recognize that within each of these worlds of experience there are diverse kinds of communities of people.

Within reservation areas, there are some communities — often more rural and more isolated — that are more traditional in their value orientations. Members of these communities tend to be less integrated with the larger society politically and economically. Unemployment and underemployment are chronic problems in many of these communities. Incomes are low and uncertain. Dependence on various kinds of assistance tends to be high.

Uncertainty is a common experience in these communities. Not only is there the uncertainty associated with poverty, but there is a sense of an uncertain future too. Federal programs and federal policy, which are in a constant state of flux, have a great impact on these communities.

Danger, in many ways, also characterizes life in these communities. The incidences of disease, ill health, and early death are high. Accidents (especially automobile) are common. The level of violence is high in comparison to many other communities. There is interpersonal violence, as well as violence related to tragic accidents. Grobsmith, writing about one such community, observes that the young in these communities are often "bored, restless, and looking for excitement. The result, all too often, is the deadly combination of alcohol, drugs, and cars. Alcoholism is a disease that plagues young and old alike" (44).

There is much ambivalence in these communities. There is often a sense of hopelessness, and yet there are moments of hope for a better future. There is much insecurity here (owing to the uncertainties and dangers of life), and yet these communities are often havens of security (acceptance and familiarity) from other communities experienced as hostile and incomprehensible. There are many contradictions, experienced particularly by the young, pushing away and pulling back the residents of these communities.

Education is often seen as a promise of a better future, but too often it has disappointing results. Again, Grobsmith observes, "Although adults want training and education for their children and encourage them to obtain the skills necessary for potential employment, most of the schooling meets the needs of literacy but falls short of preparing them for work in the non-Indian society" (44). Dropout rates are high, levels of achievement low, and undereducation is prevalent.

On the more positive side, children in these reservation communities are more likely to have access to grandparents who continue to transmit traditional values, which have survival value in this context:

> Without question, it is the intense exposure [these] children have to native life that equips them with knowledge of the indigenous culture—a situation impossible for children in [other communities on the reservation]. Learning traditional values is also an automatic part of daily life in [these communities], for the behavior of the old people is still very much in keeping with the native style. (Grobsmith 42)

On the other hand, there are other reservation communities where one finds less persistence of traditional culture and values. As Grobsmith observes, life in these communities appears similar to life in non-Indian towns. Unemployment rates are lower. Members of these communities often have the highest levels of education attained on the reservation. Their style of life often represents assimilated patterns. There is greater integration with the political and economic institutions of the larger society. Consequently, life is characterized by greater security and even (relatively speaking) affluence. Value orientations appear to be similar to those of the dominant society—again, more consistent with the community of experiences of these people.

The urban world, as noted earlier, represents the world that is increasingly the world of experience for many Native Americans. While it presents some sharp contrasts with the world of the reservation, this is not entirely the case. For many Native Americans there are many similar experiences in the urban world and the reservation world. This is so because the urban world most often experienced by Native Americans is the urban ghetto. Many of the same things that characterize life in the rural reservation communities also characterize life in these ghetto communities.

Poverty, although not as widespread in the urban areas as in the reservation areas, is still prevalent. More than a fifth (21%) of all urban Indian families have been identified as falling below the poverty level (Johnson 1974). Owing in part to lack of job skills and attained education, unemployment and underemployment are common experiences of life.

Uncertainty is also commonly experienced in these ghetto communities—uncertainty in being able to keep a roof over one's head, in finding and keeping a job, in generating income, in being able to remain in the community at all. In 1970 Robert White wrote about this experience among urban Native Americans:

> The life of these people is above all one of perpetual insecurity. One is never sure what calamity the morrow might bring, and without financial resources or prestige

within the community to command respect and protection these Sioux are at the mercy of events. Life for these people cannot be an orderly series of little events leading to a more or less predetermined goal. (187)

Danger is similarly a part of this life. White again observes:

It is a life of violent changes and violent emotional experiences. And in a life of constant violent emotional experience, no experience is felt unless it is strong. The subtle shades are not noticed, only the brightest contrasts. . . . Differences of opinion, a personal slight — all are settled immediately and physically. (187)

Ambivalence, too, is found in this kind of urban community. There is hope — the hope that initially brings many people from the reservation to the city or from one urban community to another — but there is a sense of frustration and hopelessness when those dreams fail to materialize. There is a marked absence of the security that one finds in the reservation community, reflected in the fractioning of the family. The extended family, which is a source of security in the reservation community, is less readily available in this urban community. Even the security of the individual family is not always present:

Even in the reservation society the family tended in many instances to be mother-centered because of the lack of a solid male economic role to define the husband-father role within the family. But as the Sioux men become involved in the culture of excitement, the conflict of the husband-father role with loyalties to the drinking group brings about a definite Sioux matriarchal family type. (White 187)

The educational experience of youth in the urban ghetto is often similar in many respects (especially outcomes) with that of the rural reservation community. Again, many experience system failure — underachievement, dropping out, and undereducation.

One difference, perhaps, is that the Native American student experiences an even more heterogeneous community in the urban school than in the reservation school.

Even though the urban world is physically different from the rural reservation world, there are similarities in the communities of experience of many Native Americans in these two worlds. In particular, many share the experience of danger, uncertainty, and ambiguity.

Again, it is important to bear in mind that not all Native American peoples experience the ghetto community in the urban world. There are some who have been able to find a place in stable working-class or middle-class communities in the urban world. Somewhat like their reservation counterparts who live in communities where lifestyles more approximate assimilated patterns, members of these urban communities, too, are more integrated politically, economically, and socially with the larger society. The experiences of Native Americans in these communities are often not very different from those of non-Indians who live in similar urban communities. Certainly, they experience greater economic security with respect to employment, income, and the future. They also experience fewer of the hazards and dangers encountered by those living in the urban ghetto.

What of values, then, in these varied Native American communities? What might one expect values to be like? In the rural, less integrated reservation communities, there ought to be persistence of the traditional values for many people—although those values are likely to be expressed differently than in the past. This is so because the world experienced by members of these communities is much the same as the world experienced in the past.

The dangers experienced make bravery a meaningful value today. Unfortunately, this value cannot readily be expressed as it was traditionally—in the buffalo hunt or in counting coup on an enemy. As Bryde points out, one consequence of this is that sometimes "acceptable" and sometimes "unacceptable" expressions of bravery result. Among acceptable expressions might be such things as participation in rodeo, basketball, or military service or "speaking up" for what one believes to be right. Among the "unacceptable" might be such things as drinking bouts and general recklessness.

The uncertainties experienced today by many Native Americans in their rural reservation and urban ghetto communities also make fortitude a relevant value. Since the beginning days of the reservations, Native peoples have endured incredible hardship with relatively little complaint. In fact, in terms of protest movements and movements for change, most of these had their beginnings in urban areas. People today continue to endure many hardships and deprivations with little complaint. Many stories come to mind which illustrate the continued importance of this value—children coming to school ill-clothed against the winter cold and not complaining; or saying nothing about frost-bitten ears until a teacher notices; or a teacher and her children walking to school bundled in blankets when the car could not get through an impassable driveway in the winter. Reserve can still be seen among youth in the presence of their elders much as it was in the past. Further, people must have fortitude to endure the tragedies that are a frequent part of life in these communities.

Persistent poverty makes generosity another meaningful value today. As in the past, survival depends upon cooperation and pooling of resources. It depends upon helpfulness and reciprocity. This is, in fact, well demonstrated in the observed inverse relationship between household composition and family income. The lower the family income, the larger the household—as members of extended families pool their meager resources to survive. As family income increases, the size of the household decreases.

Ambivalence and undereducation result in the wisdom from elders still being valued. There are so many contradictions encountered in everyday life that school simply does not prepare one for them—in part, perhaps, because many of those in the school do not share in that community of experiences. Under such circumstances, if there is an elder available to the young person, he may indeed be seen as a source of advice and counsel, as in the past.

For many of the same reasons—similarities in experience— one is likely to find traditional values meaningful for the rural reservation person and for the urban ghetto person. The dangers associated with the urban ghetto are supportive of the continued high valuation of bravery. The insecurity and hardships of that community call for fortitude. The poverty experienced in the ghetto community makes it sensible as well as moral to be helpful and generous. Dealing with ambivalence in the urban ghetto, however, is somewhat more problematic because access to elders is likely to be more limited. Consequently, it is suggested that one return frequently to the reservation. Failure, for some, to resolve these ambivalences intensifies problems like alcohol and drug abuse.

In contrast, the values of those in the stable working or middle-class communities and in the more integrated reservation communities are likely to be most different from those that have been considered here. They diverge the most from the traditional Native American values. Aspects of traditional values may persist, nonetheless, although not so strongly as in the other communities just discussed. Socialization (that is, how individuals were raised and what they experienced in childhood) and "identity reminders" (from kin and others) contribute to some of this persistence.

The value system of these people is more likely to include or reflect the value priorities of the dominant American culture. But, in saying this, one also needs to remember that the dominant culture is not so homogeneous as is sometimes imagined. There are class and other differences in value priorities in the dominant culture also.

In conclusion, I have proposed here that persistence vs. change in value systems is related to the communities of participation and to the communities of experience of people. There is persistence of traditional Native American values, a persistence attributable to the persistence, in some quarters, of the extended family and attributable to people's adaptation to present experiences—often marked (as in the past) by danger, uncertainty, hardship, and ambiguity. On the other hand, there is also evidence of value changes—changes in the direction of becoming similar to the value system of the dominant culture. These changes may be attributed, in part at least, to the emergence of the nuclear or individual family as the functional community unit and to

164

people's adaptation to present experiences — more often marked by security, stability, and success as defined by the larger society. Thus, Native American communities and values are interrelated — but are becoming increasingly diverse.

WORKS CITED

Bryde, John F. *Modern Indian Psychology.* Rev. ed. Vermillion, S.D.: Institute of Indian Studies, U of South Dakota P, 1971.

Byler, William. "The Destruction of American Indian Families." *The Destruction of American Indian Families.* Ed. Steven Unger. New York: Association on American Indian Affairs, 1977, 1-11.

Grobsmith, Elizabeth S. *Lakota of the Rosebud: A Contemporary Ethnography.* New York: Holt, Rinehart, and Winston, 1981.

Hassrick, Royal B. *The Sioux: Life and Customs of a Warrior Society.* Norman: U of Oklahoma P, 1964.

Johnson, Helen W. *American Indians in Transition.* Agricultural Economic Report No. 283. Washington: U.S. Dept. of Agriculture, 1975.

Kohn, Melvin L. *Class and Conformity: A Study in Values.* 2nd ed. Chicago: U of Chicago P, 1977.

MacGregor, Gordon. *Warriors Without Weapons: A Study of the Society and Personality Development of the Pine Ridge Sioux.* Chicago: U of Chicago P, 1946.

Maynard, Eileen and Gayla Twiss. *That These People May Live.* Washington: Dept. of Health, Education and Welfare, 1970.

Rokeach, Milton. *The Nature of Human Values.* New York: Free, 1973.

Wax, Murray L. *Indian Americans: Unity and Diversity.* Englewood Cliffs, N.J.: Prentice-Hall, 1971.

White, Robert A. "The Lower-Class 'Culture of Excitement,' Among the Contemporary Sioux." *The Modern Sioux: Social Systems and Reservation Culture.* Ed. Ethel Nurge. Lincoln: U of Nebraska P, 1970, 175-97.

The Pipe and Cross:

Varieties of Religious Expression in Dakota

MARTIN BROKENLEG

Father Brokenleg, associate professor of Native American studies at Augustana College, is also a member of the Rosebud Sioux Tribe and an Orthodox priest. This paper was presented at the 1985 South Dakota Humanities Seminar at Augustana College.

In the historical novel *The Way of the Sacred Tree* (1983), Edna Hong describes the cultural, military, and identity conflicts of the Santee during the 1860s. In the Lakota Kaduza and the white missionary John Williamson, Hong focuses the dynamics of culture and identity. The interaction of a white Christian and a Lakota occurs during the events we call the Minnesota-Santee War of 1862. In one section, the cultural conflict which a Santee would face, were he to become a Christian, is expressed in the words of his grandfather, Red Beaver:

> It is because the Dakota man has to give up everything that makes him a Dakota man, my son! He gives up fighting. He gives up smoking the sacred pipe. He gives up his nakedness, for the missionaries think it is shameful. He gives up the blanket, for he has to work with his hands. He gives up his long hair. He gives up feasts. He gives up the drums and dancing. If he has more

than one wife, he gives them up. He gives up his freedom to do as he pleases on the holy day. To ask a Dakota man to walk the Jesus road is like asking the buffalo to live as a beaver. (Hong 95)

In the cultural and military turmoil of the 1800s the way of life and thought of the Lakota was often questioned in the form of religious conflicts.

Our times are not unlike those times for the Lakota, although the questions continue for Native Americans. Writing in the spring, 1984, issue of *Federation Reports,* Walter Capps speaks of the way religion reflects social and cultural issues:

Every day brings new evidence that religion is a significant component of contemporary social, cultural and intellectual life on both a national and international scale. Within only the past five years, for example, a political and cultural revolution occurred in Iran, inspired and nurtured by the strong reascendency of fundamentalist forces within Islamic religion. Not far from there, the strife that persists in the Middle East is fanned by long-standing antagonisms between cultures and religions that have grown up side by side, both in continuity and in contrast to each other. The political and economic upheavals in Latin America and in developing nations throughout the world bring religious forces into sharp and violent opposition, frequently making enemies of adherents of one and the same religion. (44)

But one doesn't have to go so far away to see cultural and political changes embodied in religion. In our region we have seen the interaction of at least two vastly different cultures and religious traditions in the interplay of European Christians and native people. Although the sharp contrast between these two ways of life was manifest in the last century, it would be a mistake to think that there was nothing dramatic about their differences and similarities now. As persons are facing the dilemmas of the twentieth century, they turn to religion to provide some direction and wisdom:

167

Today more than ever before, people are trying to understand both their own and others' traditions; they are learning to appreciate that each way of life has its own value
and particular capacity to tap the creative resources of
human consciousness. As people the world over seek to
learn about the many ways in which others have related
to their immediate and to their cosmic environment, they
are turning toward American Indian tribal traditions. They
are listening to tribal wisdom that has survived in oral
tradition . . . . (DeMallie in Walker xiii)

It follows that Americans would turn to native traditions to study
since they are an integral part of American life and identity:

Native American cultures are familiar to most Americans,
being widely treated in literature, art and film. Native
Americans are inseparable from American identity — its
peoples, landscapes, arts, and history, and it is commonly recognized that rituals, ceremonials, and mythological
stories are an important part of Native American cultures.
(Gill xiii)

For this discussion I have reduced the topic of ethnic diversity
on the prairie plains to diversity of religious practice and thought
among the Lakota. I understand *ethnic* to refer to the culture
of a particular group or nation. Culture is learned and taught.
It is the pattern of life which is shared by members of a group
and which functions on four different levels. The first level is
thought, and it includes such broad areas as philosophy, theology,
values, ethics, and metaphysics. A second level of culture is speech,
which includes the language spoken and the form and content
which that expression permits. The third level of culture includes
all physical actions from ceremonies to nuance of movement.
The fourth level of culture is the physical level of culture and
includes the arts and technology of that nation. Using this defini-
tion of culture gives one the opportunity to see the various levels
on which one would find religion manifested. There would be
a philosophy of religion, a particular language and expression

168

of religion, a ritual and ceremony, and the utensils and objects used in that religion. In all the levels of culture a consistent pattern would be found.

I have used the term *pipe* to refer to the general category of the historic tribal religion of the Lakota. I mean to include those who follow a medicine man, use the pipe, participate in the sun dance, and express the spiritual sensitivity of the historic and traditional practice of the Lakota. I use the term *cross* to refer to a generic Christian, either Catholic or Protestant, who maintains the theology, faith, and outlook of the Christian expression of his or her denomination.

The traditional Plains Lakota way of life is permeated with religious practice and thought:

> No important decision was made, no important action was taken, and no important milestone in life was passed without first consulting and seeking the guidance and assistance of the supernatural . . . . The Lakota understood their world and the universe more generally to be inhabited by a multitude of supernatural beings and forces — beings and forces which were identified as "wakan" — sacred or mysterious. These beings (or spirits) and forces were many, and they were everywhere throughout the universe. They had no beginning, and they had no end. They were eternal. (Hess 17-18)

During the Plains period, Lakota religious life centered on the seven rites described elsewhere by Black Elk (Brown) and others (Walker). Some of these rites, such as the Inipi rite of spiritual strengthening, and the vision quest, are of such antiquity that their origins are not recounted in the mythic memory. But the Lakota have been the recipients of revelations with many of the remaining five rites. The Buffalo Calf Woman, who brought the sacred pipe, is also a revealer of the womanhood, ball-throwing, and soul-keeping rites. Other rites are the result of visions experienced by individual Lakotas, including the rite of the sun dance and the making-a-relative ceremony. The Plains period is characterized by religious life which is the result of spiritual revelation from the wakan.

Viewed in an anthropologic way, the Plains period demonstrates the creativity and vitality of the Lakota. As life on the plains requires adaptability for survival, so the religious life of the Lakota adapted to introduced cultural items. Whether it was the buffalo or the horse, the Lakota made it a part of Lakota life and religion.

> By the middle of the 19th century, the nomadic tribes of the Northern Plains, especially the Sioux, had developed a way of life that dominated the plains area. Their life way was linked with the horse and the buffalo, both of which had become dominant religious symbols. Their religious practices were focused upon individual vision experiences, shamanic practices associated with hunting and curing, and the great Sun Dance ceremonial, which had established itself as a tradition rooted in the primordial past. Yet from the perspective of American history, we can see that the presence of the Sioux in the Plains area and the way in which their religion had developed resulted, though indirectly, from the presence of Europeans in America; the horse, by which they had come to such great power, was itself a European introduction. This fact, of course, takes nothing away from the significance of the religions and cultures of the Plains peoples; indeed, it celebrates their enormous capacities to engage in a history of development and radical innovation that permitted them not only to survive, but to achieve heights of cultural and religious development. (Gill 163-64)

This ability to adapt would be called on by the Lakota again when the end of the known way of life seemed near. At the end of the nineteeth century, the Lakota could see that all that had supported the former nomadic life was disappearing. The land restrictions and the loss of the buffalo, the increasing presence of non-Indians, and the advent of the reservation-enforced dependency, all announced an end to the known means of life.

The Lakota responded with the adoption of the Ghost Dance with its promise of a new restoration of the complete life we had formerly known. But the promise was not then to be fulfilled. Wounded Knee would end the desperate hope in religion to restore life as it was known.

Two major dynamics would change the religious makeup of the Lakota: the plan of the Quakers, and the loss of military and political control over Lakota lives. The effect of these two dynamics would bring the Lakota to acceptance of Christianity at a time when there seemed the greatest need for it. But the acceptance of another religion would mean a conversion in culture and social position as well.

In the 1860s various Christian churches were engaged in the evangelization of Indian nations. From time to time competition appeared among the missions. The Quakers' successful work among native people was admired by the federal administration at the time of Grant's peace policy. The Quaker plan to assign specific denominations to Native American nations was therefore in effect from 1870 to 1890. Some denominations were assigned Indian schools, but the federal government took control of them by 1894. By the 1890s churches were established on all reservations and many Native Americans had become members of them:

By 1930 there were some 150,000 Indians reported to be communicants of various Christian denominations. The Catholics reported 61,456 adherents, the Protestants 80,000. Protestant missions among Indians reported a total of 26 sects and 32,164 Indians involved in these missions. Ordained Indian ministers numbered 86 among Southern Baptists, 36 Methodists, 75 Presbyterian, and 36 Episcopalian. It would appear that at least one-half of the Indians had by this time been reached and that most of these counted themselves communicants of one or another Christian denomination. Many also participated in one or another of the native ceremonies. (Spicer 119)

Note that conversion to Christianity was not necessarily to the total exclusion of participation in traditional rites. The Quaker plan was the formal, federally organized introduction of Christianity into Indian country, and its introduction had cultural implications:

> By the time of the Allotment Act, almost every form of Indian religion was banned on the reservations. In the schools the children were punished for speaking their own language. Anglo-Saxon customs were made the norm for Indian people; their own efforts to maintain their own practices were frowned on, and stern measures were taken to discourage them from continuing tribal customs. (Deloria 251-52)

The religious conversion had taken on additional aspects of cultural and social conversion and distinctions were not always clear. In identifying the motive for acculturation, Milton states, "More personally, whites have resented Indianness and have felt insulted that the Sioux did not respond eagerly to white American ways" (134).

The westernization of the Lakota was possible now since the Christian presence was in place. It only remained for the religious core of Lakota life to be drained of power. This power loss was to occur when the military, political, and economic pressure on the Lakota mounted at the end of the nineteenth century. The beginning of reservation life brought about the power loss and caused the Lakota to fill the former religious core of life with the power of Christianity:

> [There was] a diversity of religious responses on the part of Oglala leaders at a critical time in Lakota history. The years of warfare, the Ghost Dance, and the Wounded Knee massacre were still fresh and vivid memories. The Lakotas appeared to be defeated. Conversion to Christianity seemed inevitable and the conflict between Lakota religion and Christianity seemed an either-or choice. (DeMallie in Walker xviii)

Time and again, the history of this period demonstrates an absence of a distinction between the religious persuasion of the Lakota and their cultural-political persuasion. The religious loss of power occurs when there is a political loss of power. The change to Western culture is hand-in-hand with a religious change to Christianity:

> On reservations, the traditional means of attaining prestige, wealth, and rank vanished. There was no war, no hunting, and no raiding. The traditional tribal economy collapsed, and this collapse forced radical changes in diet, clothing styles, and housing. The people had no choice but to accept rations and annuities from the U.S. government, which supported them in this way while attempting to turn the people into farmers like the settlers. Because of the climate, land conditions, and temperament of the people, this effort failed miserably. The native peoples were forced to undergo political reorganization in order to have a means of meeting white demands, and this conflicted with the traditional political organization, which itself could no longer function. (Gill 165-66)

The creation of reservations usually resulted in the establishment of a mission. In some cases the mission was charged with operating schools, hospitals and farms:

> As the reservations became more permanent, the churches devoted themselves whole-heartedly to converting the people. Religious controversies increased, and missionaries soon became one of the most vocal forces in demanding that tribal political activity be suppressed, since it was apparent to them that the religious and political forms of tribal life cannot be separated. Soon plans were underfoot to ban tribal religious ceremonies. The ignorance of the Indian agents assisted the missionaries in their endeavors, since they interpreted any Indian ceremonial as a "war dance." (Deloria, *God Is Red* 251)

The effect of westernization in its many forms is stated quite clearly by Ella Deloria:

It was as though, after being sucked without warning into a remorseless whirlpool and helplessly lashed and bruised by the wreckage pounding around them, the people had at last been thrown far off to one side and were sitting there, naked and forspent, dully watching their broken life being borne along, and lacking both the strength and the will to retrieve any of it. And what good was it now anyway, in pieces? The sun dance — without its sacrificial core; festive war dances — without fresh war deeds to celebrate; the Hunka rite of blessing little children — without the tender Ring of Relatives to give it meaning — who would want such empty leavings? No, it was better just to get along somehow without. But it left them lonely, with an ache in the heart and an emptiness of soul. And then the church came and filled that emptiness to overflowing. (64)

While not minimizing the effects of the political and military loss to the Lakota, Deloria speaks of the repowering of Lakota life by Christianity in positive terms.

In a much more poignant way, Walker recorded the feeling of personal loss of one Little Wound:

These are the secrets of Hunkayapi. You must not talk of them with anyone except a Hunka or Ate. My friend, I have told you the secrets of the Hunkayapi. I fear that I have done wrong. But the spirits of the old times do not come to me anymore. Another spirit has come, the Great Spirit of the white man. I do not know him. I do not know how to call him to help me. I have done him no harm, and he should do me no harm. The old life is gone, and I cannot be a young man again. (198)

The major cultural diversity the Lakota experienced was not freely chosen by them. It came upon them as the result of history and political loss. The presence of a substitute culture and religion which reestablished Lakota power and purpose is one which continues to cause readjustment today:

As the Plains tribes entered the 20th century, they were forced to adjust to a very complex situation. Prevented from following their old way of life, they found it impossible simply to import a new tradition. Three main paths were entered by various groups, and these paths were often combined. One path was to hold to those practices that have threads of continuity with the old tradition and try to revive them as much as possible. Along this path, the Sun Dance and other ceremonial activities were eventually revived. Another path was to encourage pan-Indian identity as much as possible and to develop traditions that were "Indian" in character. Numerous political organizations and ceremonial practices like the powwow arose as a result. Another path was the attempt to drop tribal and "Indian" identity as much as possible and to assimilate completely into white culture. One step in this direction is the acceptance of Christianity and the acquisition of employment apart from the native reservations and communities. (Gill 167)

Not all would agree that off-reservation employment and the adoption of Christianity are simply means of acculturation. Gill may oversimplify the dynamics of culture and place, but he does demonstrate the conflict and diversity which westernization brings to the Lakota. Westernization does not affect only culture, nor only political status. Westernization affects the Lakota in all of these areas, and it is difficult to see any one concept in isolation from the other concept.

In the 1970s several events occurred which support the growing, conscious nationalism of the Lakota. In the 1960s in America one could see the sense of self-identity increasing among ethnic minorities. This self-identity has now spread to other groups. All around the globe there has been an increase in nationalism. In France the Basques have asserted their identity and rights. Among the native Hawaiians we have seen a resurgence of native culture and a restoration of their historic religion and deities. Among the Ukranians who were formerly Orthodox, there are groups which have discarded Orthodoxy and have returned to former deities and religious practices of the Ukraine. The resurgence of conservative Protestantism in the American white population may also be a resurgence of nationalism. Among the Lakota and other native nations, Indian activist groups organized in the sixties and seventies, confronted, sensitized, and organized. They also asserted the restoration of traditional native values and rights. They almost always insisted on the renewal of traditional religious practices:

> It is important to see how religion and world views are often deeply involved in the national idea; the advent of nationalism represents a new backdrop against which religious attitudes and world views are thrown. (Smart 49)

The importance of religion in native cultures is acknowledged by those familiar with Native American life. Perhaps because of this understanding, the U.S. Congress passed, in 1978, the Native American Religious Freedom Act (P.L. 95-341):

> [This act is designed] to protect and preserve for American Indians their inherent right of freedom to believe, express, and exercise the traditional religions . . . including but not limited to access to sites, use and possession of sacred objects, and the freedom to worship through ceremonials and traditional rites. (Gill xiii-xiv)

The act also calls for an examination of the federal policy currently in practice to determine if any changes must be made to conform to the spirit of this act (Deloria and Lytle). The act was necessary since traditional Native American religious practices have not been given the same First Amendment protections as those enjoyed by Judeo-Christian practices. Native people have experienced some challenge to the possession of materials, such as feathers and peyote; some ceremonies such as the sun dance were prohibited by the policy of the Bureau of Indian Affairs in 1883 (Gill). The interaction of the passage of the Native American Religious Freedom Act and the rise of Native American nationalism in the 1970s has created a powerful force which has brought the contemporary Lakota community to four major religious positions. It could be expected that the Lakota would develop a variety of responses to the religious and cultural history experienced. Native Americans, though characterized by a substantial communal orientation, have never had a uniform philosophy or practice. Some diversity in the religious area, or any other area, is not surprising. Moreover, the encounter with western culture and with other religious practices has not been a uniform experience for the Lakota. The contemporary organization of Lakota religious practice is neither final nor absolute. There may yet develop additional religious responses by the Lakota. Perhaps some forms will combine in the future. It is the case, however, that the question of religious practice is the most pressing personal question among native people today. In question is not only where one prays, but the implication of religion for political, cultural and social life as well. The four practices, as I see it, include: (1) those who want Traditional religion alone, (2) those who are Christian exclusively, (3) those who combine Pipe and Cross because they see no essential difference, and (4) those who combine practices for the sake of peace and unity.

There are those who believe Lakotas should practice only the Traditional historic religion. Adherents of this position may be non-Indian, but it is more likely that they will be Lakota themselves. The Traditionalists generally support Lakota language, identity, and culture but may not exemplify a uniform expertise in these areas. The Traditionalists may be from the reservation or urban centers. They usually have been somewhat embittered by their experiences with Christianity, as Giago argues:

The original missionary approach was that we are heathens, and our souls must be saved. This was the priority; education was secondary or incidental . . . . But the single most dreadful change that tore at the very core of all Indian children was the separation and isolation from our parents, grandparents, and family . . . . The system was wrong, and the system has changed, but too late for too many . . . . That so many of us have survived is a tribute to the enduring nature of our people, and this has sustained us mightily. (vii-viii)

These words are from the recollection of Tim Giago about his parochial boarding school experience. In a section titled "The Mission," Giago reflects on the result of his exposure to a church education and on the missionaries who brought it:

> Perhaps they didn't save our souls,
> But did our souls need saving . . .
> Flickering names, forgotten memories
> Of a time not so long ago.
>
> When I pass a Catholic church
> Sometimes I remember them,
> Not always with fondness, I fear.
> But I never enter the church. (6)

A clear expression of the Traditional-only type of response is published in a statement of general purpose of the Oyate Wanji Program (One People). The program organizers at the South Dakota State Penitentiary state their understanding of religion and culture:

Spiritual disturbance occurs from an absence of spirituality. This is the reason why American Indians are suffering today. Our beliefs in our sacred ceremonies are looked upon by the ignorant white peoples as pagan and improper worship of the Creator. The American Indians were introduced and sometimes imposed upon to convert into the Judaeo Christian ethics and the Gospel. We the American Indians understand that the problem is not the Gospel, but the way it is presented to the American Indians. It seems to us that the white people can take a beautiful book of Life and change all the meanings to fit their own culture and values to make a beautiful wanekia (savior) into a blue-eyed, blond Jesus with a white man's name and culture, trying to save the whole

178

world into a white culture . . . . We . . . believe that our
sacred ceremonies like vision quest are very important
in our eyes . . . with the help of Tunkasila (grandfather)
and our spiritual way of Life we can better ourselves
and make a better tomorrow. To those who are wander-
ing in confusion between two cultures and values, self-
discovery is very important to overcome identity-crises,
cultural shock, alienation, absence of spirituality, and
spiritual disturbance, to lead positive and constructive
lives . . . . We the Oyate Wanji Program with hopes and
dreams mingled with sincerity and honesty are making
a sacred journey to restore the broken hoop in our lives.
(Brings Plenty 1-3)

One has to appreciate this group's hope and vision for a future
cohesive life. They maintain that this whole life will occur with
the observance of a religiously traditional life.

A second group of Lakota believe that the best religious op-
tion is found in adherence to Christian life. Speaking in broad
terms, this group tends to be middle-aged and is more likely
to be Protestant. Among the Lakota this would imply that most
Lakota in this category would be Episcopalian, Presbyterian,
or Congregationalist. When missionaries first arrived, there was
only a slow growth of membership in Christian churches. With
time, growth in church membership increased geometrically. "A
whole new generation has grown up, educated in mission and
government schools and living according to the bureaucrats' dictates; these young Indians rigorously rejected old religious activities as a continuation of paganism" (Deloria, *God Is Red*
252). Vine Deloria, Jr., contends that it was this generation of
mission-school-educated Lakota who not only held that the old
religion was pagan but that there were Indian values and practices which had to be given up to be civilized (Deloria, *Speaking
of Indians*). Vine Deloria's aunt, writing forty years earlier, says
about the Christian lifestyle of Lakotas during World War II:

Through trouble and tears, pleasure and laughter, the
church has stood by the people and it must be said that

179

in their devotion they have stood by it too. It has meaning for them; it functions even in their social life. Never
is there a feast or an hour of games or even a political
meeting but a church service precedes it. That is habit;
it has been from the beginning. Only the other day (this
is 1944), I heard of a woman who came late to work
at a mission in western South Dakota and explained the
reason. "I was so sleepy. Lawrence was going off to war
on the early train. So we got up at three in the morning
and ate breakfast. Then his father had prayers, and then
we started for town." I know that father. He is an ordinary layman, and he never made any pretensions as
a religious leader among his people. Yet, as a matter
of course, he reads prayers before he sends his boy off
to war. (Ella Deloria 68)

Christianity came to be woven into the lives of most Lakotas.
Christian life is colored by the Lakota tendency to practice religious
ceremonies at all occasions, and it reflects the character of the
Christian denomination of the practitioner.

The Christian Lakota understands the world through Christian theology and may see traditional Lakota life through Christian theology. Gene Rolland is a member of the Body of Christ
Church at Pine Ridge and spoke about Traditionalists today and
past Lakota practices in this way:

As Moses was up there talking to God, the people were
playing around. They were making gods of gold. The
great wrath of God came upon them. When the flood
came, God's wrath came upon the people of this world.
He will destroy the world by fire since they were worshipping idols. The idols today that people are worshipping,
the Sun Dancers are worshipping the sun. People are
idolatrous, the witchcraft . . . . There is a spiritual
adulterer, serving other Gods, serving the Peace Pipe,
just like they did when Moses was up on Mount Sinai,
they are worshipping that. And it is an Abomination
unto God, that we are serving other gods. There is only

one God who created heaven and earth, which is the one God Almighty. He is the only One. (Steinmetz, "Pipe, Bible" 138-39)

The Christian Lakota is dedicated to a life as a Christian but may or may not see the value of practicing Traditional Lakota social customs. In general, the Lakota Christian outlook toward non-Indian life and people is one of openness. The Christian-only Lakota wishes to participate in Christianity but not in Traditional Lakota religion.

The remaining two categories are ways in which Lakotas and others combine practices from Traditional Lakota religion and from Christianity. The first of these combinations I term the Culturalists. By this term I mean that they see that there is only one God, one Creator. This one God is worshipped in different ways because of cultural differences. Advocates of this position hold that there are several ways or paths to one God. The Lakota and Christian paths are separate only because they originated among different peoples. Culturalists would not actually speak the words attributed to them, but by their actions and assumptions the conclusion is clear.

The Culturalist position is similar to the current ecumenical position of many Christian churches. My experience has been that most of the Culturalists are, or have been, influenced by the Catholic Church. Indeed the practices of many Catholic clergy and laity seem to be modeled on the Catholic philosophy of ecumenism. Ecumenism uses the approach to variant practices as a difference in rites. That is, the distinctive traditions are only ceremonial and not essential. In church settings, Rome speaks of western rite and eastern rite and so on. The differences which exist are due to history and culture. The Culturalist, too, maintains that the Cross and Pipe differences are due to culture and history.

Father Steinmetz ("Pipe, Bible") would perhaps liken the Culturalist category to his Ecumenist One distinction among the Oglala. He understands that the Ecumenist One sees Christianity and Lakota Traditional religion as alternatives for particular settings. I mean the Culturalist position to include blends of

Traditional religion and Christianity but to differ from Steinmetz. The Culturalist can combine Cross and Pipe at one and the same time. History and culture are the only differences between them since there is only one God worshipped. Father Steinmetz also defines an Ecumenist Two position as an Oglala who sees the Pipe as a Christian object and the Bible as becoming Lakota. My category of Culturalist allows for either the position one or two of Steinmetz to be included in either the Culturalist heading or the next category we will consider. An example of a Culturalist is found in the conversation of Ben Black Elk with Father Steinmetz:

> During most of my life I was in doubt about the relation between the Pipe and Christ. When I believed in the Pipe, was I betraying myself as a Christian? What was the meaning in my life of interpreting my father's life to John Neihardt and Joseph Brown? But now I see that the Pipe and Christ are really one, the doubts of conscience of many years are ended and I have a deep spiritual peace. (Steinmetz, *Meditations* 142)

Ben Black Elk, the "fifth face" of Mount Rushmore, speaks of his fundamental conviction that the Pipe and the Cross are really the same, that there is ultimate unity beyond the differences which are perceived. Another example of a Culturalist is the Reverend Mitchell Whiterabbit, who says, "I like to think of Indian tribal religions as other roads leading us to God the Ultimate Being, the Creator of all good things, the Sustainer of us all" (Coffman 21).

The fourth Lakota response to religious differences is also a response which permits the adherent to combine the way of the Pipe and the way of the Cross. The response of the Diplomat is a more traditionally Lakota response. It ignores any real discussion of what it is that separates the two religious practices. The Diplomat may believe that there is some ultimate unity but is more likely to simply begin from the difference between Pipe and Cross. The conclusion which is stressed is that there must be a unity for the sake of peace. Steinmetz, while seeming to be a Culturalist, speaks of results of combining Pipe and Cross. Mutual respect and deep involvement are the benefits for the participants from both religions:

> John Iron Rope, a Catholic medicine man, gave his approval when I prayed with the Sacred Pipe at the funeral of Rex Long Visitor. This was the beginning of many friendships. Frank Fools Crow, the leader of the tribal Sun Dance for many years, was delighted that a Catholic priest prayed with the Sacred Pipe . . . . Pete Catches, Sr., formally a Catholic catechist, was my spiritual director of my Vision Quest. (*Meditations* 7)

> Mass was celebrated in 1969 on the Sun Dance grounds following the piercing ceremony after the flags in the four directions had been removed. Edgar Red Cloud, the leader of the Sun Dance singers sang a Sun Dance song, holding the Sacred Pipe during the distribution of Holy Communion. Frank Fools Crow who performed the piercing a short time before received Holy Communion with Edgar Red Cloud and George Plenty Wolf. (*Meditations* 138)

Clearly one of the major consequences of working together in spite of fundamental differences is the unity and goodwill which the Diplomats seek. One does not need to seek for differences since they are just beneath the surface. It is difficult for Native Americans to keep alternate value systems in balance:

> A great many Indians reflect the same religious problem as do the young whites who struggled through the last decade of social disorder. They are somehow forced to hold in tension beliefs that are not easily reconciled. They have learned that some things are true because they have experienced them, that others are true because everyone seems to agree that they are true, and some things they feel are insoluble and cannot be solved by any stretch of the imagination. (Deloria, *God Is Red* 259)

183

The goal of seeking peace and goodwill is the overriding concern of those who wish to combine Pipe and Cross. A medicine man, Richard Moves Camp, speaks of the interaction and mutuality of the Cross and Pipe having divine origin:

> After the Buffalo Calf Woman brought the Pipe, a white man came dressed in a buffalo robe speaking Lakota and blessed the Pipe. This was Christ who came in the spirit before the white men brought Him. I believe that this was Christ coming in the Spirit to the Indian people at the same time He was born among the white man. This vision is the reason why I respect all the Christian Churches. (Steinmetz, *Meditations* 143)

These four responses to the religious and cultural questions raised by the Pipe and Cross display the remarkable diversity of religious expression among the Lakota. The four positions are not combined and should not be. The Christian-only and the Traditional-only groups defy combining, and the motivation for the Culturalists and Diplomats who combine is varied. The diversity of religious expression influences other aspects of life: values, social relationships, and political preferences. The religious practices of the Lakota are clearly examples of ethnic diversity, diversity in culture and pattern of life.

One of the mottos of the United States is *e pluribus unum:* out of many, one. The choice of this motto is apt since the emphasis in our country has been to unify the diverse people who make up the American citizenry. It has many benefits — chiefly, a reduction in conflict among diverse ways of life. This is only one kind of social experiment, however.

Canada, with its new constitution, has announced a different direction with its policy of support for cultural diversity on all levels. The great risk in advancing the uniqueness of the many that make up Canada is that the differences will become conflicts, and that the conflicts will become unmanageable. Canada has already experienced conflict over language and subsequent political division. The contemporary Lakota response to religious difference is the decision to permit diversity. The Lakota are familiar with the similarities between the Pipe and Cross, but also with the contrasts between them. The Lakota historical experience has shown the influence which religion has on other aspects of culture. The Lakota experience may be only a forecast of conditions which citizens of this country and continent will face in times to come. It is already the case that most of us have encountered people different from ourselves more often than was common in times past. It seems clear that the future of religious life will occur within the global community (Smart).

The question the Lakota have faced is the choice of requiring a uniformity for the sake of peace, or permitting diversity at the risk of conflict. In relating to Western culture in America, native people have clearly been directed by its governmental, educational, and religious institutions to conform. Now the entire country, and even the globe, faces the same question of uniformity for the sake of peace, or diversity at the risk of conflict. This question has been answered among the Lakota with diversity at the risk of conflict. It is not yet clear how the United States will respond to the Lakota in the future.

While I have understood the philosophical question raised by the Lakota experience with religious diversity, I have not communicated the ways this question appears in daily life for Lakotas. A Lakota faces the question of uniformity or diversity with everyone he meets. Every personal interaction with family, friends, and strangers occurs with this issue near the surface. Whether the exchange is with non-Indians or other Lakotas, Pipe and Cross and their cultural implications are near. The Lakota response may forecast the religious and ethnic future we face. Ninian Smart, author of *Worldviews: Cross Cultural Exploration of Human Beliefs,* makes this prediction:

> . . . the great religious traditions will more and more ask themselves what the meaning of their past is in view of the present unification of the globe. There may still be dreams in some religions of becoming, so to say, the church of the whole globe . . . . But it seems more plausible that religions will function more as denominations and sometimes as sects. They will be denominations in

185

the sense that they will live together with a certain mutual recognition, but perhaps feeling that it has the right slant on life, but not altogether excluding the visions and values of the other traditions. Each will strive to bear witness to its own true self, and to spread such light as it possesses, but without the real hope of becoming the exclusive faith of all the world. Because such a tolerant attitude is in some degree threatening to the authority and certainty of the past, the backlashes in each faith will take the form of global sectarianism. The conservative and traditionalist response to pluralism is to reaffirm the exclusive rightness of one's tradition and one's revelation. (167-68)

WORKS CITED

Brings Plenty, L. *Sobriety Through Traditionalism*. Sioux Falls, S.D.: SDSP-Oyate Wanji Program, 1985.

Brown, J. E. *The Sacred Pipe: Black Elk's Account of the Seven Rites of the Oglala Sioux*. New York: Penguin, 1983.

Capps, Walter H. "Religion, the Great Teacher." *Federation Reports* 7.2 (1984):44-46.

Coffman, M. R., ed. *Alive Now* 14 (1984):5.

Deloria, Ella C. *Speaking of Indians*. Vermillion, S.D.: Dakota P, 1979.

Deloria, Vine, Jr. *God Is Red*. New York: Grosset and Dunlap, 1973.

Deloria, Vine, and C. M. Lytle. *American Indians, American Justice*. Austin: U of Texas P, 1983.

Giago, Tim A. *The Aboriginal Sin*. San Francisco: Indian Historian P, 1978.

Gill, Sam D. *Native American Religions*. Belmont, Calif.: Wadsworth, 1982.

Hess, D. J. *Faith as a Way of Life*. Indians of North America: Readings for Anthropology 421. Brookings, S.D.: South Dakota State UP, 1984.

Hong, Edna. *The Way of the Sacred Tree*. Minneapolis: Augsburg, 1983.

Milton, John R. *South Dakota: A History*. New York: Norton, 1977.

Smart, Ninian. *Worldviews: Cross Cultural Exploration of Human Beliefs*. New York: Scribner's, 1983.

Spicer, Edward H. *A Short History of the Indians of the United States.* New York: D. Van Nostrand, 1969.

Steinmetz, P. B. "Pipe, Bible and Peyote among the Oglala Lakota: A Study in Religious Identity." *Stockholm Studies in Comparative Religion* 19 (1980):1-188.

— — —. *Meditations with Native Americans — Lakota Spirituality.* Sante Fe, N.M.: Bear, 1984.

Walker, James R. *Lakota Belief and Ritual.* Ed. Raymond J. DeMallie and Elaine A. Jakner. Lincoln: U of Nebraska P, 1980.

THE EDITORS

HARRY F. THOMPSON, archivist at the Center for Western Studies, is a former Dixon Wecter Graduate Fellow in American Studies at Baylor University. He also holds graduate degrees in English from Colgate University and the University of Rochester and has taught composition and literature at the University of Rochester, Winthrop College, and Augustana College. He has had articles published on American literary publishing houses in *The Dictionary of Literary Biography* (Bruccoli Clark/Gale Research, 1986) and on the historical collections at the Center for Western Studies in *South Dakota History*. He is also the author of *The Archives and Manuscripts Collections of the Center for Western Studies* (1984) and *Guide to the Archives of the South Dakota Conference of the United Church of Christ* (1987). He is currently directing the History of the Arts in South Dakota Project.

ARTHUR R. HUSEBOE is professor of English at Augustana College and chairman of the Humanities Division. One of the founders of the Nordland Heritage Foundation, he has also served as its president and currently is the executive director. His research and writing interests have been in two rather different areas: Western American literature and English comedy of the later seventeenth century. He has edited and co-edited several collections of essays about the literature and history of Siouxland and the Middle Border: *Where the West Begins* (1978), *Big Sioux Pioneers* (1980), *Siouxland Heritage* (1982), and *The Prairie Frontier* (1984). He wrote the introduction to the reprinting of Frederick Manfred's *Scarlet Plume* (Nebraska, 1983) and is co-editing the letters of Manfred for the University of Nebraska Press. He is the author of the monograph *Herbert Krause* (Boise, 1985) and an article on Herbert Krause and Ole Rölvaag in the forthcoming study *A Literary History of the American West* (Texas Christian University, 1987). Dr. Huseboe's work on Restoration comedy includes a number of essays and two books: *Sir John Vanbrugh* (G. K. Hall, 1976) and *Sir George Etherege* (G. K. Hall, forthcoming). He has also served for eight years as a member of the South Dakota Committee on the Humanities.

SANDRA OLSEN LOONEY is professor of English at Augustana College, where she teaches both Western and Eastern literature and freshman composition. Active in the Nordland Heritage Foundation, she has been project director of the Berdahl-Rölvaag Lecture Series several times over the past years. She is co-editor of *The Prairie Frontier* (1984). Dr. Looney also reads selections from regional literature each morning on "Under Cover," a radio program produced by KRSD (Sioux Falls), a Minnesota Public Radio station.

THE ARTIST

CARL GRUPP is associate professor of art at Augustana College, where he teaches drawing, painting, and printmaking. He has participated in over one hundred regional, national, and international exhibitions, and his work is found in such collections as the Minneapolis Institute of Art, the Chicago Art Institute, the American Embassy in London, the Pillsbury Company Collection, the General Motors Corporation Collection, and many college and private collections.

THE NORDLAND HERITAGE FOUNDATION PUBLICATIONS

The Nordland Heritage Foundation supports and promotes the study and preservation of Scandinavian — particularly Norwegian — heritage on the Prairie Plains. Since 1975 the Nordland Heritage Foundation, in conjunction with Augustana College and the Sioux Falls Scandinavian community, has sponsored annually the Nordland Fest. Further information concerning the Nordland Heritage Foundation and its publications may be obtained by writing to:

The Nordland Heritage Foundation
Box 2172, Humanities Center
Augustana College
Sioux Falls, SD 57197